# Internal control and accounting systems

## Tutorial

Michael Fardon

**osborne
BOOKS**

© Michael Fardon, 2010. Reprinted 2011, 2012.

Published by Osborne Books Limited
Unit 1B Everoak Estate
Bromyard Road
Worcester WR2 5HP
Tel 01905 748071
Email books@osbornebooks.co.uk
Website www.osbornebooks.co.uk

Design by Laura Ingham
Cover and page design image © Istockphoto.com/Petrovich9

Printed and bound by CPI Group (UK) Ltd, Croydon, CR0 4YY

British Library Cataloguing in Publication Data
A catalogue record for this book is available from the British Library

ISBN 978 1905777 389

# Contents

# Acknowledgements

The author wishes to thank Maz Loton and Cathy Turner for their help with the production of this book. The author is also grateful to Jo Osborne and Roger Petheram of Worcester College of Technology for contributing practical ideas and advice about the delivery of the course. The publisher is particularly grateful to the two students who have kindly given permission for the use and adaptation of original Report material which appears in this text.

The publisher is indebted to the Association of Accounting Technicians for its help and advice to our authors and editors during the preparation of this text and its permission to reproduce the Sample Assessment included in this book.

# Authors

**Michael Fardon** has extensive teaching experience of a wide range of banking, business and accountancy courses at Worcester College of Technology. He now specialises in writing business and financial texts and is General Editor at Osborne Books. He is also an educational consultant and has worked extensively in the areas of vocational business curriculum development.

# Introduction

## what this book covers

This book has been written specifically to cover the Learning Area 'Internal Control and Accounting Systems' which combines two QCF Units in the AAT Level 4 Diploma in Accounting:

■ Principles of Internal Control

■ Evaluating Accounting Systems

This book is different from other Osborne Books AAT Tutorials in that it is more of a handbook for the Learning Area rather than a series of traditional chapters with activities.

It is based on the fact that the student has a choice of two assessment methods:

• writing a report based on workplace evidence

• writing a report based on an AAT Sample Case Study

These two assessment methods have a number of requirements in common which are covered by a sequence of separate chapters in the book. These common requirements are:

• learning about the the theoretical aspects of organisations, accounting systems, legislation, regulations and fraud

• analysing and reviewing an accounting system

• writing a formal report

The book also contains sample material for both assessment routes:

• an AAT Sample Case Study

• two sample student reports

## International Accounting Standards (IAS) terminology

In this book the terms set out below are quoted as follows, ie IAS terminology (UK terminology):

income statement (profit & loss account)

inventory (stock)

statement of cash flows (cash flow statement)

statement of financial position (balance sheet)

trade payables (creditors)

trade receivables (debtors)

# 1 Introduction to internal control and accounting systems

*This first chapter is an introduction to the Learning and Assessment Area 'Internal Control and Accounting Systems.'*

*The chapter will explain:*

- *the reasons why this Learning and Assessment Area is rather different from any other you will have encountered so far in your studies*

- *the two possible assessment methods – using workplace evidence or a written Case Study – and what they involve*

- *what will be expected of you as you complete the Learning and Assessment Area*

- *how to organise your method of working to make the most of your resources – and especially your time*

- *the need to map the assessment criteria*

## INTRODUCTION TO THE LEARNING AND ASSESSMENT AREA

### what this Learning and Assessment Area involves

The Learning and Assessment Area 'Internal Control and Accounting Systems' combines two separate units:

- **Principles of Internal Control** – which is based on the the way in which the accounting function operates within an organisation and the need for an effective internal control system

- **Evaluating Accounting Systems** – which involves evaluating an accounting system – based either on workplace evidence or a Case Study – and making recommendations for the improvement of that system

### what you will learn

When you have completed this Learning and Assessment Area you should be able to:

- **understand the role of an accounting system** in an organisation in supporting different departments of the organisation and dealing with outside organisations and individuals

- understand the importance and principles of **internal control** of the accounting function in an organisation – to help efficiency and to prevent the incidence of fraud

- **evaluate an accounting system** in a real-life situation or in a Case Study by:

    - identifying the requirements of the accounting system

    - working out the improvements that could be made

    - making suggestions as to how the improvements could be implemented

    - identifying the impact the changes would make on the system and its users

### your assessment – the Report

The assessment will take the form of a **formal Report** (3,500 to 4,000 words) submitted electronically to AAT for marking by your training provider, who will be required to ensure that all areas for assessment have been covered.

This Report can be based on:

- your findings from an actual **workplace,** or

- an AAT **Case Study**

Your tutor will be able to advise you to choose which of these two options to take – workplace evidence or Case Study.

Whatever you decide to do, you will find that this is where this Learning and Assessment Area differs in its assessment from most of the other assessments you will have encountered so far in your studies. It is not difficult, but it is challenging and it is different.

You will find that your studies will give you the opportunity to take on a new role – almost that of a consultant – and you can be creative in your approach and thinking. The content of your report should:

- **review a current accounting system**, focusing on record keeping systems, principles of internal control, current methods of fraud prevention, and working methods and training

- **analyse a current accounting system**, identifying weaknesses or areas where improvement could be made and making recommendations to improve the system, bearing in mind all the costs involved

## WHAT YOU WILL NEED TO DO – AN OVERVIEW

This section is intended to give you an idea of what you need to do in order to write your Report. It is not exhaustive and you are recommended to discuss these requirements with your tutor.

### initial research and setting the scene

To start with, you should:

- give a **description of the organisation**, which could be a real workplace or based on a Case Study

- define the structure, purpose and organisation of the **accounting function** within the overall organisation

- identify the **relationship** between the accounting function and the other internal departments

- identify the important **external relationships** the organisation maintains; this could include relationships with customers, suppliers, shareholders, banks, trade organisations and governmental bodies such as HM Revenue & Customs

- decide **what an organisation requires from its accounting systems** – these requirements will differ depending on the nature and size of the organisation and will often be based on computer software solutions

### review of the accounting system

You will then need to **review the accounting system** to ensure that it meets the requirements of the organisation. In short . . .

- how good is it?

- do things go wrong?

- could things go wrong?

This review involves:

- identifying the **strengths and weaknesses** of the accounting system – this should include a review of the working methods used within the accounting system to ensure that the best results are being achieved especially in terms of cost-effectiveness, reliability and speed

- describing the **external regulations** that will influence the way the accounting system will operate (eg legislation affecting payroll, or VAT regulations)

- deciding **which areas of the accounting system you will evaluate** – including, for example, sales, purchases, credit control, banking, payroll, petty cash, budgeting and management reporting; if it is  a small organisation with a simple structure you could cover a number of these; if it is a larger, more complex, organisation, just one or two areas may be evaluated

- **reviewing and evaluating the internal control system** by identifying areas where there is a potential for **error**

- **reviewing and evaluating the internal control system** by identifying areas where there is a potential for **fraud** involving loss of money, stock or working time, and then assessing the level of risk of that fraud – ie how likely it is

- identifying **ways of detecting fraud** and the types of **internal controls** that could be established to prevent fraud occurring

- **reviewing the weaknesses** that have been identified and explaining their impact upon the organisation – in terms of time, money and reputation (for example the loss of revenue, time wasting, letting customers down)

### making recommendations

You will need to be able to make clear and sensible recommendations to improve the weaknesses identified in the evaluation of the accounting systems:

- for every weakness identified you must make **at least one recommendation** for improvement.
- if you have identified just **one weakness** within an accounting system then you should compare **two or three possible solutions** and state, with reasons, which solution you believe to be the best
- you should work out the **comparative cost** of the recommendations you are making, for example the cost of training, new computers, and the benefits they will provide; the need for staff training is particularly important

## THE LEARNING PROCESS IN THIS BOOK

The processes described so far – and the thought of writing a report – may seem daunting, but when you have finished this chapter you should be much more familiar with what is required and see how it all fits together.

There are three processes involved – the three 'R's:

**Research** the workplace (or **R**ead the Case Study)

**R**eview the accounting system

**R**ecommend improvements

### learning the theory – research and read

In order to be able to assess an organisation and its accounting system you will need to acquire basic knowledge about areas such as:

- types of organisation – their needs and links with the commercial world
- accounting systems – their areas of activity and how they link with the rest of the organisation
- internal control systems
- fraud and risk
- cost benefit analysis – how to assess the benefits of a recommendation in relation to its costs

All these theoretical areas are covered in the chapters that immediately follow this one. These are:

**Chapter 2    Organisations and accounting systems**

This will explain the way in which accounting systems work and how they support the organisation and how they relate to outside bodies.

**Chapter 3    Internal control systems and fraud**

This will explain the way in which an organisation and its accounting system should exercise internal control over all its operations and so avoid the incidence of errors and fraud.

## reviewing the system and recommendations

When you are confident of your knowledge in these areas, you will then be able to

- **review** an accounting system
- make **recommendations** for improvement
- assess the benefits of a recommendation in relation to its **costs**

This is covered in:

**Chapter 4    Reviewing systems and making recommendations**

This will explain how you can review and evaluate an accounting system and carry out a cost benefit analysis – assessing the benefits of each recommendation in relation to its costs

## the report

At this stage you will be ready to write your report. This is covered in

**Chapter 5    Writing the report**

This will explain all you need to know about structuring and writing the text of a formal report.

As noted earlier this report can be based on:

- your findings from an actual **workplace,** or
- an AAT online **Case Study**

In order to show you what is required by these two forms of assessment we include at the end of the book:

- a sample AAT Case Study
- sample student reports based on workplace evidence

## THE REPORT

The basis of your assessment is a 3,500 to 4,000 word Report, often referred to as 'The Project,' which is the culmination of your project work, which has to be submitted online to your assessor.

It is our aim in this book to make the writing of this Report as smooth and painless as possible. In most cases you will have people to help you both at your training provider and also at your workplace (if you have one), and you also have this text to fill in the gaps in your theoretical knowledge.

The diagram on the opposite page shows you the processes that you will normally go through to successfully produce your **workplace evidence** – to complete the Report and answer any extra questions that may be required to complete coverage of the assessment criteria of this Learning Area. Please study it carefully and then read the notes that follow.

If you are using the **AAT Case Study** instead of workplace evidence, the processes will be similar, except that most of the evidence will be provided for you and you will have **a limit of four months** for final completion of the Report.

### finding a 'workplace' or using an AAT Case Study

One of the most difficult parts of preparing for the Report is making initial decisions. You will have to decide what organisation (if any) you are going to use as a basis for your Report and what areas of that organisation you are going to write about. If you are working in an organisation or do voluntary work in an organisation you will be able to gather **workplace evidence**. If you are an accounts manager or working in an accounts department, life is made easy for you, but if you are currently not working and are studying to get a qualification to enable you to work, this option may not be open to you. All workplace evidence that you provide must be:

- **valid** – it must be relevant to your investigation
- **authentic** – it must be real
- **current** – it must relate to current practice
- **sufficient** – there must be enough of it

If you find that there is not enough scope in your chosen organisation to provide all the evidence you need, your assessor may ask you to answer **additional questions** and submit the answers online.

As noted above, if you do not work in an accounting environment, or at all, you may wish to take advantage of the **AAT Case Study** assessment method.

## suggested assessment plan – using workplace evidence

**choosing workplace**
or other organisation
to assess
as the basis of the report

**choosing subject area(s)**
within the accounting system
- evaluating system
- planning and evaluating possible
changes to the accounting system

**using experience**
- in workplace
or
- situations described in
AAT Case Study

**AGREE SUBJECT WITH ASSESSOR**

**consulting with people**
- workplace mentor
or manager
- training assessor
- timescale
- content
- resources needed

**THE FIRST 500 WORDS**

**learning from this book**
- about the format and
style of the report
- about what you need to
include in the report
- the theory of
organisations, accounting
systems, internal control
and fraud

**DRAFT REPORT COMPLETED**

**mapping**
checking that the report
covers the assessment
criteria

**assessor interviews**

**producing extra evidence**
to cover the assessment
criteria not covered in
the report

**FINAL REPORT SUBMISSION**

### choosing a subject

The next decision to be made is the subject of your Report. In a nutshell, you will need to find an area in an accounting environment – eg payroll processing, paying suppliers, cash handling, job costing – which could be improved so that its processes become more efficient and less open to error and to fraud.

If you are in work, this should be straightforward, as you will have time to look around. If you are not in work, your training provider may be able to arrange for you to do work experience or to work shadow. Time for investigation will be more limited here, but you should be able to decide on a subject for the Report.

If you are not in work, or if work experience or work shadowing are not possible, you should then identify an organisation such as a club or local charity which will be able to help, or twist the arm of a friend or family member who has access to a workplace or organisation. An area for investigation in the accounting function can then be identified.

### consulting with people – your mentor and assessor

It is important that, if you are in employment, you establish a relationship with a **mentor** (advisor) in the workplace who will be able to help you gather evidence and who will eventually be able to certify your work. This mentor might be a line manager or a more senior manager.

If you are not in work, you will have to find someone who is. This person will then become your 'mentor' and source of information.

You will also need to identify your **assessor** at your training centre. He or she should provide you with support, discussing with you the subject of your Report and monitoring its progress as you compile the evidence.

Whatever subject you choose, it should be agreed both with your employer or contact and also your assessor (eg your college tutor).

### learning from this book

In order to make the most of this textbook, you should:

- start by reading Chapters 2 and 3, which will provide you with the theoretical background for your investigations
- then read Chapter 4, which will explain how you can review and evaluate an accounting system and carry out a cost benefit analysis – assessing the benefits of each recommendation in relation to its costs

- study Chapter 5 which will explain about the format of the Report, help you to choose the subject to be covered and make sure that you understand the assessment criteria that have to be covered

then,

- make the most of the sample student reports which should give you an idea of what you should be aiming at for workplace evidence assessments

and, if you are taking the Case Study route . . .

- study the sample AAT Case Study and analyse the simulated workplace evidence which it will contain

## time schedule

The diagram on page 9 proposes a schedule for the writing and the assessment of the Report which could be completed in approximately eight months by part-time students. This is only a suggestion – drawn up after consultation with a number of AAT teaching centres. Note that AAT allows four months for the writing and electronic submission of a Report based on the AAT Case Study. The workplace evidence route allows more flexibility.

## MAPPING OF ASSESSMENT CRITERIA

An important part of the assessment process is the coverage of the assessment criteria of the two units of the Learning Area 'Internal Control and Accounting System':

- **Principles of Internal Control (PIC)** which sets down the requirements for the areas of knowledge that you will need

- **Evaluating Accounting Systems (EAS)** which involves developing your skills in evaluating an accounting system

These are set out on the next two pages, together with page references to where they are covered in this book.

In your Report you will need to map the assessment criteria covered. You should refer to your tutor for the method you should adopt for this.

The important requirement of your assessment is that you should cover **all** the assessment criteria. It may be that this will not be possible in your Report, because of the scope of the Report. Your tutor will tell you how to 'fill the gaps' so that you can complete some further written work and complete the assessment requirements.

**PRINCIPLES OF INTERNAL CONTROL (PIC) – COVERAGE OF ASSESSMENT CRITERIA**
Note: the numbers in brackets refer to the page numbers in this book.

**Learning outcome 1:**

**Demonstrate an understanding of the role of accounting within the organisation**

1.1　Describe the purpose, structure and organisation of the accounting function and its relationships with other functions within the organisation. (21-22)

1.2　Explain the various business purposes for which the following financial information is required (26-28)

• income statement (profit and loss account)

• forecast of cash flow (cash flow statement)

• statement of financial position (balance sheet)

1.3　Give an overview of the organisation's business and its critical external relationships with stakeholders. (16)

1.4　Explain how the accounting systems are affected by the organisational structure, systems, procedures, and business transactions. (18,23)

1.5　Explain the effect on users of changes to accounting systems caused by

• external regulations (33)

• organisational policies and procedures (34)


**Learning outcome 2:**

**Understand the importance and use of internal control systems**

2.1　Identify the external regulations that affect accounting practice. (33-34)

2.2　Describe the causes of, and common types of, fraud and the impact on the organisation. (38-41)

2.3　Explain methods that can be used to detect fraud within an accounting system. (42-43)

2.4　Explain the types of controls that can be put in place to ensure compliance with statutory or organisational requirements. (35)


**Learning outcome 3:**

**Be able to identify and use the appropriate accounting system to meet specific organisational requirements**

3.1　Identify weaknesses in accounting systems (54-56)

• potential for errors

• exposure to possible fraud.

3.2　Explain how an accounting system can support internal control. (52-53)

3.3　Identify ways of supporting individuals who operate accounting systems using (59)

• training

• manuals

• written information

• help menus

3.4　Explain the value and benefit to a specific organisation of different types of accounting systems and software packages. (57-58)

**EVALUATING AN ACCOUNTING SYSTEM (EAS) – COVERAGE OF ASSESSMENT CRITERIA**

Note: the numbers in brackets refer to the page numbers in this book.

**Learning outcome 1:**

**Evaluate the accounting system and identify areas for improvement**

1.1    Identify an organisation's accounting system requirements. (15-16)

1.2    Review record keeping systems to confirm whether they meet the organisation's requirements for financial information. (51)

1.3    Identify weaknesses in and the potential for improvements to, the accounting system and consider their impact on the operation of the organisation. (54-59)

1.4    Identify potential areas of fraud arising from lack of control within the accounting system and grade the risk. (41-46)

1.5    Review methods of operating for cost effectiveness, reliability and speed. (52-53)

**Learning outcome 2:**

**Make recommendations to improve the accounting system**

2.1    Make recommendations for changes to the accounting system in an easily understood format, with a clear rationale and an explanation of any assumptions made. (65-75)

2.2    Identify the effects that any recommended changes would have on the users of the system. (59)

2.3    Enable individuals who operate accounting systems to understand how to use the system to fulfil their responsibilities. (59)

2.4    Identify the implications of recommended changes in terms of time, financial costs, benefits, and operating procedures. (60-62)

# 2 Organisations and accounting systems

## this chapter covers...

*In this chapter we examine the way in which the accounting function 'fits into' the overall structure of the organisation and how it relates to other organisations.*

*The areas the chapter covers include:*

- *the way in which what an organisation does – its 'business' – affects its accounting function*

- *the influence of the external stakeholders of the organisation*

- *the overall structure of the organisation*

- *the structure of the accounting system*

- *the way in which the accounting system interacts with the other functions*

- *the administrative systems and control of resources within the organisation*

- *the uses of the financial statements of the organisation*

- *the effect on an accounting system of changes brought about by external regulations and internal policies and procedures*

*You will see from these topics that this material forms much of what should go into the introductory and analysis sections of your Report.*

*Project writing hints are provided within the text of the Chapter.*

## THE 'BUSINESS' OF THE ORGANISATION

### public and private sectors

Organisations are normally classed as public sector or private sector.

**Public sector organisations** are those owned or controlled directly or indirectly by the state. They include corporations like the BBC, Government Departments and local authorities. Their function is largely to provide some form of service: broadcasting, health, education, policing, refuse collection, tax collection, for example. Some public sector organisations form partnerships with private sector companies to provide a service, eg hospitals in the National Health Service.

**Private sector organisations**, on the other hand, are in private ownership, and include businesses ranging from the sole trader to the public limited company. The function of these organisations is to provide a product such a car or TV or a service such as a holiday or a foot massage.

The range of activities carried out by both public and private sector organisations – the nature of their 'business' can therefore be classified as:

- providing goods – either through manufacturing or through retailing
- providing a service – either for consumers (private sector) or as a social benefit (public sector)

You may not consider that tax collection is a social benefit, but if you appreciate that tax revenue is used for Government spending on health and education, you will see the logic.

### how the 'business' affects the accounting system

All organisations need accounting systems to carry out the accounting function. This function includes:

- processing and recording financial transactions – keeping accounts
- payroll
- costing and budgeting
- raising finance

You will see from this list that these are 'generic' functions which are common to all organisations. The variation is in the detail and will depend on the type of 'business' the organisation carries out:

- a manufacturing company in the private sector, for example, will keep accounts for suppliers and customers, will run payroll and will cost and budget for the manufacturing process and other activities; it is likely to raise finance from banks and possibly the equity markets

- a local authority in the public sector will keep accounts for suppliers and
to a lesser extent for customers, it will run payroll and keep to strict
budgets; its financing, however, will come from Central Government,
local enterprises and from local taxation

---

**Report writing hint**

When you write about the accounting system of your chosen organisation
you will need to relate the system's functions to type of activity carried out
by the organisation – its 'business'.

---

## DEALING WITH EXTERNAL STAKEHOLDERS

**A stakeholder is a person or organisation that has an 'interest' in
another organisation.**

Stakeholders can be **internal** (eg employees, managers) or **external** (eg
shareholders, banks, customers, suppliers, the tax authorities). Your
assessment requirement covers the relationship with the **external
stakeholder**s of an organisation.

Take for example a retail organisation such as an electrical supermarket
chain which is also a public limited company quoted on the stockmarket.

The functioning of the accounting system will be affected by external
stakeholders in a number of ways:

- **customers** will need to be provided with easy and efficient means of
making payment, and in suitable circumstances, credit terms and finance

- **suppliers** will need to be paid on time and credit terms and discounts will
need to be negotiated and administered

- **banks** that are lending money to the company are likely to require regular
(eg monthly) management accounts, eg levels of sales, inventory, cash
held, payables, receivables

- the **tax authorities** (HM Revenue & Customs – a Government agency)
will require calculation and payment of Corporation Tax, Value Added
Tax and collection of Income Tax and National Insurance through the
PAYE system

- **shareholders** will require information about the financial performance of
the company in the form of an annual financial report in paper format or
downloadable from the company's website

- **trade associations** will request financial statistics such as sales trends, details of exports, wage rates and so on for their regular trade reports

The relationship of an organisation with its internal and external stakeholders is shown in the diagram set out below.

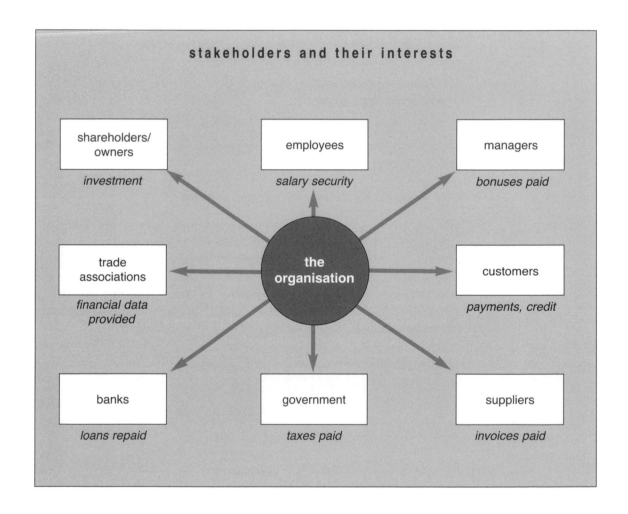

**Report writing hint**

When you write about the accounting system of your chosen organisation you will need to identify external stakeholders who place demands on the activities of the accounting system and who affect financial decisions.

## ORGANISATIONAL STRUCTURE

The organisation of the accounting system will depend a great deal on the way in which the organisation as a whole is structured.

In the case of a smaller organisation such as a private company the structure will be based on the shareholder directors being in charge of the whole business, with possibly a finance director in charge of the finance and accounting function. The variation arises when the organisation is larger, in which case the structure is likely to be either

- a loosely organised group of independent operating units, directed by a managing company, or

- driven from the top and tightly controlled as a single unit

These are represented by the two basic types of organisational structure: flat and hierarchical.

### flat structure – large organisation

This is where operating divisions of an organisation are relatively independent, and are likely to have their own accounting systems. A typical example is where groups of companies are divided up in terms of geographical areas or products. It must be stressed that it will be the responsibility of the managing company to ensure that the accounting systems of the separate companies are harmonised and work together. Study the diagram below.

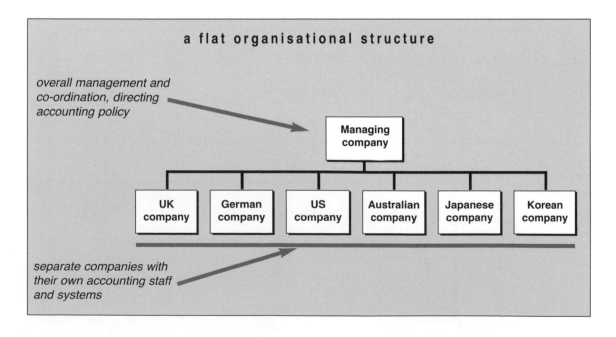

### hierarchical structure – large organisation

A hierarchy is a series of levels of people, each level controlled by the level above it. This structure – also known as a 'tall' structure – is suitable for a large organisation such as a public limited company or Government Department which may have thousands of employees. In this type of structure the accounting system will be the responsibility of the Finance Director and is centralised and strictly controlled. Study the diagram below

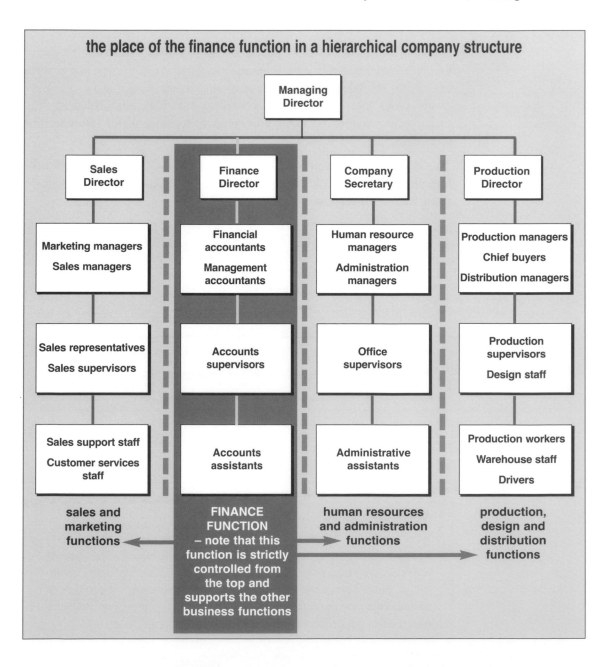

**the place of the finance function in a hierarchical company structure**

Managing Director

| Sales Director | Finance Director | Company Secretary | Production Director |
|---|---|---|---|
| Marketing managers<br>Sales managers | Financial accountants<br>Management accountants | Human resource managers<br>Administration managers | Production managers<br>Chief buyers<br>Distribution managers |
| Sales representatives<br>Sales supervisors | Accounts supervisors | Office supervisors | Production supervisors<br>Design staff |
| Sales support staff<br>Customer services staff | Accounts assistants | Administrative assistants | Production workers<br>Warehouse staff<br>Drivers |
| sales and marketing functions | FINANCE FUNCTION – note that this function is strictly controlled from the top and supports the other business functions | human resources and administration functions | production, design and distribution functions |

## organisational structure – small business

It is appreciated that this chapter has so far concentrated on large organisations. It is more than likely that the workplace you decide to study, or the scenario provided in an AAT Case Study, will be **smaller businesses** or **voluntary organisations**. The large majority of businesses in the UK are, in fact, small businesses with fifty or fewer employees.

The organisational structure of a small business is therefore more likely to be 'flat' with the boss at the top and a variety of 'functions' or small departments under his or her direct control.

One of these functions will, of course, be the **accounting function**. This may involve a line manager who oversees a number of assistants and reports directly to the business owner. It may also be the case that the business owner looks after some of the accounting functions himself/herself, for example negotiating discounts and credit terms with major customers or completing the VAT Return.

This is the type of business which features in the **AAT Sample Case Study** reproduced in this book (see page 82) and the type of business which is illustrated in the diagram below.

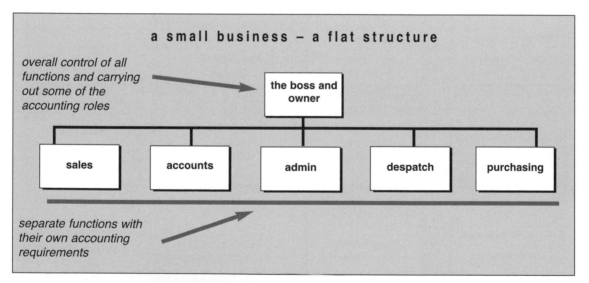

**a small business – a flat structure**

overall control of all functions and carrying out some of the accounting roles

the boss and owner

sales     accounts     admin     despatch     purchasing

separate functions with their own accounting requirements

---

**Report writing hint**

When you describe the accounting system of your chosen organisation in the beginning of your Report you will need to identify the type of organisational structure used as it may help to explain problems within the accounting system. For example, a flat structure may lead to lack of co-ordination between different functions, and a hierarchical structure may lead to poor communication between the different levels.

## FUNCTIONS OF AN ACCOUNTING SYSTEM

Your studies require you to look critically at the existing accounting system and to identify areas for improvement in both the system itself and the way in which it is managed.

A typical accounting system carries out a number of functions, shown in the diagram below. It is the responsibility of the management to ensure that it operates smoothly.

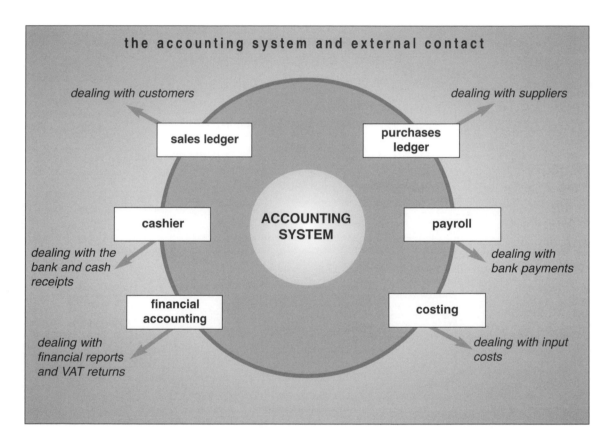

It is important that the accounting system is not seen to operate in isolation. Part of your assessment requirement is to analyse the way in which the accounting system integrates with the other internal functions of the organisation.

If the organisation is a manufacturing business, these other functions might include production, human resources, sales and marketing, administration.

Study the diagram on the next page to see how the accounting system inter-relates with some of the other internal functions of the organisation.

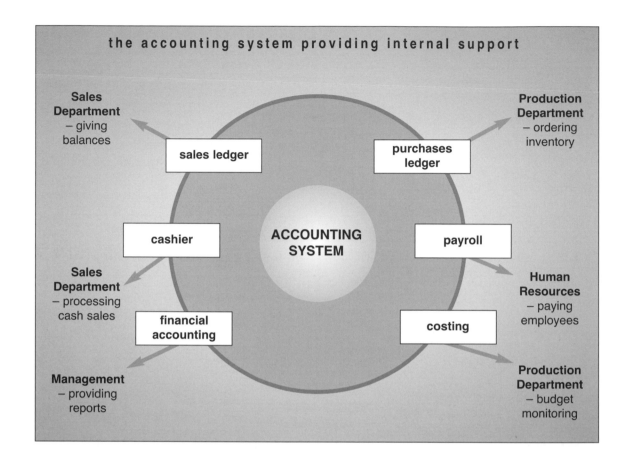

**Report writing hint**

When you write about the accounting system of your chosen organisation you will need to analyse the way in which the organisation structures its accounting system. Some form of structure chart would be a useful aid, and could be included within the Appendices.

The analysis might identify weaknesses in the way the system is structured, in the way it is managed and in the way in which it communicates with people – eg customers or suppliers – **outside** the organisation.

The analysis should also look at the way in which the accounting system deals with other functions **inside** the organisation. A good starting point is to look at communications between the various departments. Is the system at fault at all?

## THE NEED FOR GOOD COMMUNICATION

### lines of communication in an accounting system

When studying the workplace you have chosen or the scenario in the AAT Case Study you will need to analyse the effectiveness of the communication between people in the accounting function itself – in addition to the communication between people in other functions, eg sales.

The diagram below illustrates the lines of communication between accounting employees in a large company. The accounting system here is subdivided into the areas of financial and management accounting.

The boxes with the dark grey background all represent specific accounting roles. You will see that the structure is set out in a series of layers of authority and responsibility.

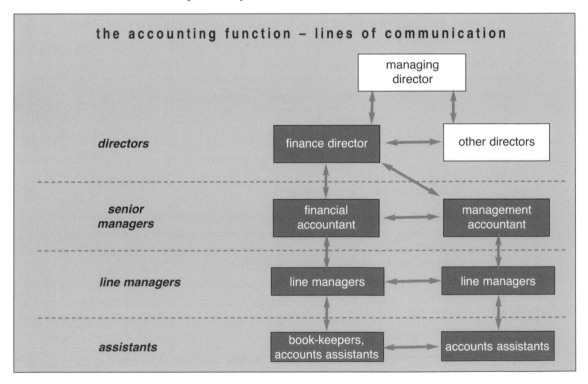

### management information systems

A large organisation is often served by a **Management Information System (MIS).** This is a computer-based system which provides up-to-date, accurate and relevant information to management. An efficient MIS will enable management to make informed decisions promptly.

By 'management' we mean all levels of management, from line managers (supervisors) through to the Finance Director. Clearly the type and level of information required will vary according to the role of the manager and the type of decision expected of that manager. Examples of the type of data produced by an accounting MIS include:

- sales figures for products and regions

- inventory (report) levels

- customer account details, ranging from balances to detailed reports such as the Aged Debtor Analysis

- budget reports showing variances

- profitability reports by product

You will see from this range of information that decision-making can range from 'Do we allow this customer any more credit?' through to 'Do we continue to manufacture this product?'

---

**Report writing hint**

When you write about the accounting system of your chosen organisation you will need to assess the MIS, if it is available. Does it enable management to make the required decisions? Is it communicated effectively within the accounting system? Can it be improved?

---

## CONTROL OF RESOURCES BY INDIVIDUALS IN THE ORGANISATION

### the need for resources

Adequate **resources** are essential to the functioning of an organisation. All come at a cost. Resources can be classified under four main headings:

- **equipment and material resources**

  These include premises in which to work and equipment needed on a day-to-day basis. They also include the materials that may be used – raw materials, inventory and consumables such as biros and photocopy paper. A car manufacturer will clearly have a greater need for equipment and material resources in a factory than a firm of insurance brokers working from a town centre office. The important point here is that in both cases the resources will need to be adequate.

- **human resources**

  This term is now used widely to describe the 'people' function in organisations. There is always a need for the right number of appropriately skilled people to work within an organisation, whether in a management or an operational role.

- **information**

  This is an essential resource and must be readily available to whoever needs it within the organisation. Computer-based systems with up-to-date and accurate information are the ideal solution (see last section). Information in a manufacturing or retail business, for example, will include product specifications, prices, inventory levels, customer orders, supplier orders. A travel agency will need different types of information, but equally, the data will need to be accurate and up-to-date and on computer screen.

- **financial resources**

  This term means 'money' which is either available currently or can be made available within a set time period to allow spending in line with a particular budget allocation. This is probably the most critical type of resource for the functioning of the organisation. It affects all areas.

## control of resources by individuals

As part of your investigation you should examine the way in which individuals within the organisation control the supply of the various resources described above. Control of resources is normally dictated by the various levels of budget within an organisation.

For example, the production or staffing budget of a business is likely to be decided upon at director level and the departmental budget will be the responsibility of the departmental manager. Line managers (supervisors) will also have decisions to make about control of resources – for example they may be given the power to allow staff to work overtime and to order small items of office equipment. Employees at assistant level will also have control of resources at a reduced level, for example ordering stationery items or tea and coffee for the rest room. It is all a question of level and scale.

The diagram below sets out the hierarchy of individuals who will make decisions about controlling resources; it shows 'level and scale'.

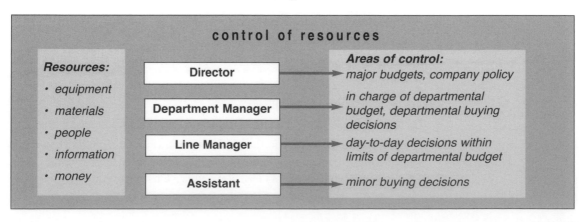

### errors and fraud within the system

The control of resources brings with it the opportunity both for error and for fraud. Both can be avoided with the enforcement of checking and monitoring procedures. **Error** includes situations involving over-ordering of matcrials – for example ordering 5,000 suspension files instead of 100 where the units ordered were boxes of 50 rather than individual files. **Fraud** is a fact of life where control of resources is concerned. It can range from a director siphoning off funds by 'fiddling the books' to the supposedly  innocent pilfering of biros and stationery at assistant level. The issue of fraud is covered in detail in the next chapter.

> **Report writing hint**
>
> When you write about the accounting system of your chosen organisation you will need to identify the individuals who control resources, and comment on the scope of the decisions they can make and the control mechanisms that exist.
>
> You should look for areas in which efficiency in the control of resources and information provision could be improved.

## THE USE OF FINANCIAL STATEMENTS

As you will know from your studies, organisations produce financial statements on a regular basis. The number and extent of the financial statements will depend on the type and size of the organisation. Preparation of the data for these statements is all part of the regular accounting work carried out by an organisation, although normally the final statements will be produced by the organisation's accountants.

The main statements produced are:

- **income statement** (profit and loss account)
- **statement of financial position** (balance sheet)
- **statement of cash flows** (cash flow statement) – not to be confused with a cash budget

Financial statements are produced:

- for **internal use** by the organisation for planning and budgeting reasons
- for **external use** to provide financial information to stakeholders such as shareholders, banks, suppliers, pressure groups, possible investors and Government bodies such as HM Revenue & Customs

We will now summarise these uses and provide some illustrations.

## financial statements for internal use

**Financial statements** – and the **ratios** that can be extracted from them – provide management with information about the financial state of the organisation. They will enable the management to analyse past performance and also, in the **master budget**, project future performance.

Areas of particular interest to senior management include:

| | |
|---|---|
| **income statement** | • sales performance |
| | • gross and net profit margins |
| | • comparison of areas of expense |
| **statement of financial position** | • liquidity |
| | • gearing |
| | • return on capital employed |
| **statement of cash flows** | • explanation of changes in the cash position of a company |
| | • investments made in assets |
| | • sources of financing |

## financial statements for external use

**Financial statements** – and the **ratios** that can be extracted from them – are also very important sources of information for external stakeholders who need to assess the financial position of the organisation. For example:

• **Banks**

  When lending, banks need to assess the financial performance and financial strength of an organisation. They need to make sure that any lending can be repaid and also that there are sufficient assets available for security. They will want to see, in the case of a limited company:

  – an income statement to verify that profit is being generated

  – a statement of financial position to ensure that a company is not over-geared (ie there is not too much borrowing already in relation to equity)

  – a cash budget to confirm that the company will have adequate cash flow over the next twelve months

• **Suppliers**

  The credit control function of many suppliers requires sight of the accounts of prospective customers – either directly or through credit reference agencies – so that they can carry out ratio analysis before granting credit terms.

- **HM Revenue & Customs**

  The income statement will provide the source of the data for the calculation of tax due on profits made.

- **Shareholders and investors**

  The published accounts of public limited companies contain the income statement, statement of financial position and the statement of cash flows. These and the investment ratios they provide enable owners of shares and prospective investors to assess the return they are likely to make on the company shares.

Extracts from the financial statements of a quoted public limited company are shown below. The money amounts are quoted in £ millions.

## income statement

| | | | |
|---|---|---|---|
| Operating profit | | **3,457** | 3,169 |
| Share of post-tax profits of joint ventures and associates | 13 | **33** | 110 |
| Finance income | 5 | **265** | 116 |
| Finance costs | 5 | **(579)** | (478) |
| Profit before tax | 3 | **3,176** | 2,917 |
| Taxation | 6 | **(840)** | (779) |
| Profit for the year | | **2,336** | 2,138 |
| | | | |
| Attributable to: | | | |
| Owners of the parent | | **2,327** | 2,133 |
| Minority interests | | **9** | 5 |
| | | **2,336** | 2,138 |
| | | | |
| Earnings per share | | | |
| Basic | 9 | **29.33p** | 27.14p |
| Diluted | 9 | **29.19p** | 26.96p |

## statement of financial position

| | | | |
|---|---|---|---|
| Financial liabilities | | | |
|   Borrowings | 21 | **(11,744)** | (12,391) | (5,972) |
|   Derivative financial instruments and other liabilities | 22 | **(776)** | (302) | (322) |
| Post-employment benefit obligations | 28 | **(1,840)** | (1,494) | (838) |
| Deferred tax liabilities | 6 | **(795)** | (676) | (791) |
| Provisions | 26 | **(172)** | (200) | (23) |
| | | **(15,327)** | (15,063) | (7,946) |
| Net assets | | **14,681** | 12,906 | 11,873 |
| Equity | | | |
| Share capital | 29 | **399** | 395 | 393 |
| Share premium account | | **4,801** | 4,638 | 4,511 |
| Other reserves | | **40** | 40 | 40 |
| Retained earnings | | **9,356** | 7,776 | 6,842 |

## statement of cash flows

| | | | |
|---|---|---|---|
| Cash flows from operating activities | | | |
| Cash generated from operations | 31 | **5,947** | 4,978 |
| Interest paid | | **(690)** | (562) |
| Corporation tax paid | | **(512)** | (456) |
| Net cash from operating activities | | **4,745** | 3,960 |
| Cash flows from investing activities | | | |
| Acquisition of subsidiaries, net of cash acquired | | **(65)** | (1,275) |
| Proceeds from sale of property, plant and equipment | | **1,820** | 994 |
| Purchase of property, plant and equipment and investment property | | **(2,855)** | (4,487) |

**Report writing hint**

If you are not able to identify the use of financial statements in the accounting system you are investigating you may need to cover this assessment criterion (PIC 1.2) in additional material provided, eg an Appendix. You should ask your tutor about how to go about this.

## CHANGES BROUGHT ABOUT BY EXTERNAL REGULATION

Very often the smooth running of an accounts system can be disturbed by forces outside the control of the organisation. Changes may be required because of the introduction of new external regulations or changes to existing rules.

Whatever the case, the accounting system should be ready to react to any external changes and have the **internal policies and procedures** established and in hand in order to be able to deal with them. Examples include:

- **a change in accounting terminology**

    You will know from your studies that there is move away from UK accounting terminology to international terminology which has been established by the International Accounting Standards Board (IASB) through its IASs and IFRSs. These are applicable to EU companies listed on a stockmarket. It is likely that this terminology will eventually supersede the existing UK terminology, meaning that more and more organisations over time will need to refer to 'receivables' rather than 'debtors' and to 'inventory' rather than to 'stock.'

    Organisations will need to amend much documentation and invest in staff training to cope with these changes. Again, internal policies and procedures will need to be established to deal with this.

- **a change in Company Law**

    Company law in the UK changed with the passing of the Companies Act 2006. This affected the way in which limited companies operated and included provisions which affected their accounting systems. For example, the requirement for authorised share capital was abolished – this affected the statement of financial position (balance sheet).

    Companies will therefore need to be alert to this type of change in legislation.

- **a change in the VAT rate**

  This can seriously disturb the smooth running of any VAT-registered business. It particularly affects retail businesses, involving the repricing of goods on the shelf and in the warehouse, reprinting of catalogues, amendments on the website, amendments to invoicing software and the training of staff to deal with a confused public.

  Most large retailers will have internal policies and procedures in hand to deal with this situation.

  Set out below is an email illustrating the way in which the accounting system is affected by a change in VAT rate and the way in which it will have to communicate with other functions in the company to advise the implications of the change.

---

**EMAIL**

To:          All Departmental Managers

From        Alex Rowlands, Finance Director

Subject:    Increase in standard rate VAT from 17.5% to 20% w.e.f. 4 January

---

As you will know, standard rate VAT is due to increase from 17.5% to 20% on 4 January.

It is essential that you all carry out the necessary procedures to ensure that the changeover goes smoothly and that our customers are aware of the price changes. I would like to highlight a number of key areas to you:

1  Accounts Department: Sales and Purchases Ledger should ensure that the Sage settings for VAT on invoices and credit notes are amended to 20%.

2  Accounts Department: Management Accounting Section should ensure that the Excel spreadsheets for cash budgets are amended to show the increase in output VAT received.

3  Marketing and Sales: all publicity literature quoting VAT inclusive prices should be withdrawn before 4 January and revised prices calculated and quoted on new publicity material. The website should be similarly checked for prices and the VAT rate on the online shop amended accordingly from 4 January.

4  Warehouse and shop: any price stickers or barcodes on stock showing pre-increase prices should be removed and replaced by new price stickers and barcodes.

Please ensure that in each case detailed instructions are issued to your staff. These instructions are available as standing instructions in the Company Procedures Manual.

Regards

Alex Rowlands

## inspiration page – for your notes

# 3 Internal control systems and fraud

## this chapter covers...

*This chapter starts where the last chapter finished, by dealing with the external regulations that affect accounting practice. Some of these are required by legislation and affect areas such as taxation, auditing and the regulation of limited companies.*

*Others are 'accounting standards' set both in the UK and internationally by independent accounting standards bodies.*

*The main part of this chapter explains the internal control systems that are set up in an organisation to implement all the requirements of these external regulations and also to detect errors and fraud.*

*The chapter describes:*

- *the different types of fraud that can be committed within an organisation*

- *the risk of fraud occurring within an organisation*

- *the areas vulnerable to fraud*

*It also explains the need to design a system so that fraud*

- *is minimised*

- *can be easily detected*

- *can be dealt with as appropriate*

# EXTERNAL REGULATIONS AFFECTING ACCOUNTING PRACTICE

## legislation

The term 'legislation' covers a wide range of regulations based on UK Acts of Parliament and European Directives. Organisations are affected by a number of legal regulations affecting the way in which an accounting system operates. Examples include:

- **taxation regulations** – affecting areas such as:
    - PAYE for individuals on the payroll: income tax, National Insurance and other deductions
    - Value Added Tax: VAT returns, invoice format, rates applied
    - corporation tax paid by limited companies

- **company law** – set out in the Companies Acts – requires that company accounts (of larger companies) should be audited; financial statements are to be drawn up in a set format and sent to shareholders; larger companies also have to send full versions of these accounts to Companies House where they can be accessed by the public

- **data protection law** – set out in the Data Protection Act 1998 – protects data (including financial data) relating to individual customers

- **late payment law** – set out in the Late Payment of Commercial Debt (Interest) Act 1998 – allows suppliers to charge interest on late payment of invoices

## UK and international accounting standards

The **Financial Reporting Council** (FRC) is a unified, independent regulator which:

- sets, monitors and enforces accounting and auditing standards
- oversees the regulatory activities of the professional accountancy bodies
- regulates audit
- promotes high standards of internal regulation within companies ('corporate governance')

The membership of the Council includes wide and balanced representation at the highest levels from the business, investor, professional and other communities interested in corporate reporting and governance.

The FRC promotes good financial reporting through its subsidiary boards, which include the **Accounting Standards Board** (ASB), the **Financial Reporting Review Panel** (FRRP) and the **Auditing Practices Board**.

The FRC now takes a more active role in relation to the internal regulation of companies, ensuring that they comply with company law, accounting standards, and auditing standards.

**Accounting standards** have been developed by the **Accounting Standards Board,** a subsidiary board of the FRC to provide the rules, or framework, of accounting. The intention has been to reduce the variety of alternative accounting treatments. This framework for accounting is represented by **Statements of Standard Accounting Practice** (SSAPs) and **Financial Reporting Standards** (FRSs).

As you will know from your other studies, large quoted companies in the European Union (including UK plcs) are required to prepare their final accounts in accordance with **International Accounting Standards** (IASs). It is anticipated in the long run that international accounting standards will eventually replace the UK Standards for all but the smallest businesses.

**International Standards on Auditing** (ISAs) are also gradually being introduced which will set down guidelines for the way in which UK businesses are audited.

## THE NEED FOR POLICIES AND PROCEDURES

**External** regulations – such as legislation – are only of any use if an organisation regulates its employees and keeps them up-to-date by issuing formal internal sets of rules and guidelines. These are often referred to as **Policies and Procedures**.

### what do Policies and procedures cover?

Illustrated on the opposite page is an internal document issued by a large company outlining the introduction of new Policies and Procedures for the retention and disposal of records throughout the business.

'Records' can be paper-based or electronic. In this case, the document produced by each function in the business – sales, administration, accounting and finance – will set out:

- what records should be retained and at what level of security – ie if they should be locked up or not
- the period of time for which the records should be stored
- what records should be disposed of (ie shredded or wiped from a computer storage medium)

In the case of the **Accounting and Finance** function, this could include:

- retention of financial documents such as invoices, bank statements, payroll records – often for six years

- safe disposal of these records after this period

- immediate safe disposal of confidential details such as credit card details from customers sent in with mailed orders

In this document the need for new Policies and Procedures is made clear:

> "The company is obliged under information legislation to have retention/disposal schedules for all its corporate records. Without clear retention/disposal policies the company risks falling foul of the Data Protection Act, Freedom of Information Act, and Public Record Act."

---

### RECORD RETENTION AND DISPOSAL – NEW POLICIES AND PROCEDURES

Our Policies and Procedures are the main reference material for people in each Department.

All formal procedures and work systems are outlined in these documents which give managers and staff the rules and guidelines.

The company is obliged under information legislation to have retention/disposal schedules for all its corporate records. Without clear retention/disposal policies the company risks falling foul of the Data Protection Act, Freedom of Information Act, and Public Record Act. Failure to dispose of records in a timely and efficient manner can lead to criticism from the Information Commissioner and Adjudicator.

Currently, information relating to how long we should be keeping records is scattered throughout operational guidance. Quite often this retention/disposal information is out-of-date and/or the reasons behind why particular time periods were chosen have been forgotten.

The people making decisions regarding retention/disposal timescales need to understand the different reasons that may effect their decision.

These new Policies and Procedures:

- lay down the company policy for documenting retention information

- explain why a retention policy is needed

- identify numerous reasons that can effect the retention period decision, and contain a good practice guide on how to construct a retention schedule

---

**Report writing hint**

When you write about the proposed change to the accounting system of your chosen organisation you will need to provide evidence that it takes account of any change in external factors such as changes in the law (eg company regulation, tax rates) and changes in accounting standards.

## INTERNAL CONTROL IN AN ACCOUNTING SYSTEM

Any accounting system will have certain elements in common, whether it is a company Accounts Department, a Local Authority Purchasing Department or a charitable organisation's fundraising section. It will:

- deal with money – handling cash
- need to make payments and issue cheques
- have 'levels of authority' within the system
- need to make decisions over ordering and purchasing
- need to set budgets for spending
- need to organise its accounting records

Unless the management is happy to let everything become totally disorganised, the accounting system will need to establish various **rules and regulations** which will establish an **internal control system,** for example:

- the establishing of **money limits** for certain transactions
- the definition of **levels of responsibility** for **authorising** transactions
- the need for **referral of decision making** to another person when required

Illustrated on the opposite page are extracts from a **Policies and Procedures** internal control document issued by the Accounts and Finance Department of a medium-sized business. Read through this and you will see that there are a number of examples of the three areas of internal control outlined above. These have been extracted and are shown below.

---

**money limits**

All orders of £1,000 or more must be authorised by the budget holder.

All cheques for £1,000 or over require two signatories.

Petty cash will be topped up on the 'imprest' system, where the amount spent is reimbursed. It is intended for small items, up to £20.

**authorisation**

All invoices must be authorised for payment by the budget holder.

Salary payments require the signature of the Accounts Manager or Financial Controller, plus one other.

**referral to another person or higher authority**

Budget holders will discuss with the Financial Controller appropriate parameters, plus maximum allowed deviations before the budget holder or senior manager is brought in; this will be documented.

Finance must be informed if there are queries delaying authorisation (of payments) or if payment is to be withheld for any reason.

---

**POLICIES AND PROCEDURES STATEMENT– ACCOUNTING AND FINANCE (extracts)**

**Books of account and records**

Proper accounting records will be kept. The accounts systems is based around computer facilities, using Sage and Excel, but manual/paper records will also be used if appropriate. The following records will be kept:

- Appropriate control accounts (bank control, petty cash control, VAT control, salary control)
- Monthly trial balances
- Petty cash and bank accounts will be reconciled at least monthly
- VAT returns produced on the required quarterly cycle

**Ordering supplies and services**

Budget holders can place orders for goods or services within their budget areas, subject only to cash-flow restraints. All orders of £1,000 or more must be authorised by the budget holder, except for specific areas of expenditure where written procedures have been agreed. Under £1,000, the budget holder may delegate all ordering as appropriate. Budget holders will discuss with the Financial Controller appropriate parameters, plus maximum allowed deviations before the budget holder or senior manager is brought in, which will be documented.

**Payment authorisation and Purchases Ledger**

All invoices must be authorised for payment by the budget holder, although the actual checking of details may be delegated. The authorising department is responsible for checking invoices for accuracy in terms of figures and conformity with the order placed, that the services or goods have been received, and following up any problems. Finance must be informed if there are queries delaying authorisation or if payment is to be withheld for any reason.

A Purchases Ledger is operated by Finance. All incoming invoices are to be passed to Finance section as soon as they arrive. Invoices will be recorded in the Purchases Ledger within two days, unless there are coding problems. They are then passed on to budget holders for authorisation. Once authorised as above, suppliers will be paid within the appropriate timescale.

**Cheque writing and signing**

Signatories will only be drawn from senior staff and directors, and any new signatory must be approved by the directors before the bank is notified. All cheques for £1,000 or over require two signatories. Cheque signatories should check that the expenditure has been authorised by the appropriate person before signing the cheque. Salary payments require the signature of the Accounts Manager or Financial Controller, plus one other. Cheques should be filled in completely (with payee, amount in words and figures, and date) before cheques are signed.

**Handling of cash**

Petty cash will be topped up on the 'imprest' system, where the amount spent is reimbursed. It is intended for small items, up to £20. Anything over this should be paid by cheque where possible. The imprest has a balance limit of £250. The petty cash balance will be reconciled when re-storing the imprest balance, or monthly if this is more frequent. All cash collected from Finance will be signed for, and receipts will be issued for all cash returned.

**Report writing hint**

When you are investigating an accounting system in the workplace, try to obtain access to the relevant Policies and Procedures document. It may not be called precisely this, but may be set out as an operations manual or even separate sets of instructions for each section of the system, eg purchasing, petty cash or sales invoicing.

## reviewing the accounting system

Your review of an accounting system, whether it is in the workplace or set out in an AAT Case Study will be covered in full in the next chapter.

You will need to appreciate that if an accounting system has weaknesses it will be because the internal control system – as seen on the previous two pages – will be deficient in one way or another. This will lead to various possible problems:

- **errors being made** because people do not know the correct way of doing things
- errors being made **and not being picked up** because the processes are not being checked properly

and lastly . . .

- **fraud being committed** because the internal control system is deficient and the opportunity for fraud is there for the taking

# TYPES OF FRAUD

## human nature?

Fraud is an unfortunate fact of life within organisations, and some would say it is part of human nature. It sometimes hits the headlines, as when a merchant banker's PA diverted over £1 million of her employer's funds into designer clothes, cars, speedboats, and general high living. Amazingly, this went undetected for a long time.

Another fraud which has now become legendary is the Robert Maxwell case in which company pension funds were raided to finance the publishing mogul's private spending.

But fraud is also taking biros and stationery or inflating a travel claim. This may not hit the headlines, but the principle remains the same – dishonesty.

It is the responsibility of the management of an organisation to:

- identify areas where the **risk of fraud** exists and to grade the seriousness of the risk in each case

- set up **control system**s involving all staff to alert management to possible occurrence of fraud

- **monitor** those control systems on a regular basis to ensure that they are working

- **deal with** any incidence of fraud in an appropriate way, whether it be a formal warning or calling in the police

These will be dealt with in the course of this chapter. First, however, it is important to define what we mean by 'fraud'.

## some definitions

Fraud covers a variety of offences, but a general definition of fraud is:

**the use of deception with the intention of obtaining an advantage, avoiding an obligation or causing loss to someone else or to an organisation**

Fraud is a criminal activity and is covered in the UK by a number of laws:

| | |
|---|---|
| **theft** | dishonestly taking someone else's property (Theft Act) |
| **false accounting** | dishonestly destroying, defacing, concealing or falsifying an accounting record for personal gain or to cause loss to someone else (Theft Act) |
| **bribery and corruption** | taking or giving a bribe that might influence the actions of others (Prevention of Corrupt Practices Acts) |
| **deception** | obtaining property, money, services or evading liability by deception (Theft Act) |

In practical terms fraud is normally a combination of any of the following:

- **theft** of property or money or information (eg someone raiding the petty cash)

- **falsification** of records so that property or money is passed to the wrong person (eg someone 'fiddling' the payroll)

- **collusion** – ie a 'set-up' between an employee and someone else outside the organisation, eg false invoices sent in by an outsider for supplies that were never made and authorised and paid by the person 'on the inside'

### examples of fraud

There are many examples of fraud which are made public. Students involved in the public sector would find it useful to look at the HM Treasury Fraud Reports, available as downloads from the website www.hm-treasury.gov.uk. These contain examples of fraud in local authorities and Government departments. Types of fraud in the private sector are very similar. The examples below have been adapted from cases reported by a leading insurance company.

---

**REPORTED CASES OF FRAUD**

**Theft of fuel stocks – *Total Loss £25,000***

A local authority had their own fuel pumps for supplying their motor vehicles. The employee in charge stole fuel over a long period as the inventory checks were inadequate.

**Payroll fraud: fictitious employees – *Total Loss £10,000***

The manager of an industrial cleaning company invented bogus employees, put them on the payroll and then cashed their pay cheques.

**Bank deposits: teeming and lading – *In 10 months a total of £7,000 was stolen.***

A clerk in charge of a sub post office stole cash receipts due to be paid into the local bank. This was covered up by delaying paying in at the bank and altering the paying-in slips relating to subsequent deposits. Stealing money received from one source and then using money received from other sources to cover it up is known as 'teeming and lading'.

**Cheque printing machine – *Total Loss £25,000***

A ledger clerk responsible for making regular payment of rent for advertising was in charge of a machine that printed cheques. Numerous small cheques were made out by him for the correct amounts but payable to him. It was several months before complaints from creditors, (who had not received their cheques) were investigated and the fraud uncovered.

**Collusion: stock control system – *Total Loss £1 million***

A well known national company was defrauded by two gangs of employees working at the same location. The losses involved collusion between warehousemen and drivers who used the spare capacity on vehicles to remove goods from the depot. False information was entered into the computerised inventory control system and their activities were only discovered when the police reported finding large amounts of the particular product in the hands of third parties.

**Collusion: fictitious sub-contractors – *Total Loss exceeded £500,000***

A major contractor with well established control systems to approve payments were the victims of fraud by a section supervisor in collusion with a computer operator. Cheques were made out to fictitious sub-contractors and despatched to private addresses.

**Report writing hint**

When you write about your analysis of the current accounting system of your chosen organisation you will need to provide evidence that you have investigated potential areas of fraud. You will need to be aware of the various types of fraud that can be committed.

# RISK ASSESSMENT AND FRAUD

## risk assessment – the role of management

Assessment of **fraud risk** is part of the **risk assessment** process which is the responsibility of organisations in both the private and the public sectors.

In the case of limited companies (private sector), the Turnbull Report has stated that directors have responsibility for ensuring that risk management practices are established as part of an effective internal control system.

In the public sector the guiding document to fraud risk is HM Treasury's 'Managing the Risk of Fraud – a Guide for Managers' available as a download from www.hm-treasury.gov.uk

The assessment of risk generally by management follows a number of distinct stages. This process applies equally to the assessment of fraud risk:

- setting up a risk management group and identifying objectives
- identifying the areas of risk of fraud
- grading the scale of the risk in each case
- developing a strategy to manage that risk
- setting up systems to detect and deal with fraud, allocating responsibility
- getting the systems up and running
- monitoring the running of the system

## the internal control system

A robust internal control system is essential if management is going to be able to detect and deal with fraud.

There are various techniques that can be used for making an internal control system 'fraud resistant':

- **fraud staff**

  Some very large organisations may appoint employees – eg ex-bank or ex-police staff – to work full-time on fraud prevention and detection.

- **management responsibility**

  Managers should be given specific areas of responsibility and answerability – eg sections of the Accounts Department – to ensure that fraud is kept to a minimum.

- **management supervision**

  Management – particularly line management – should supervise accounting activities on a regular basis. This involves overseeing and checking activities such as data entry to computers, making payments and payroll processing.

- **segregation of duties**

  The system should be set up so that duties which, when combined, could lead to fraud, are given to different people – ie they are segregated. For example, the cashier taking in cash for a business should ideally not be the same person who makes out the paying-in slip for the bank. The danger is that some of the cash may disappear into the cashier's pocket.

- **lock & key**

  Physical security – locking valuable items away – is a sure deterrent to theft. This does not only apply to cash: the tendency of items such as laptop computers and mobile phones to disappear has become a well-known and ever-increasing statistic.

- **authorisation**

  Some accounting activities may require authorisation by a nominated official. This ranges from the authorisation of petty cash, signing of cheques over a certain amount to the investing of liquid funds, eg placing £250,000 on a money market account. Clearly the larger the amount, the more senior the person giving authorisation.

## detecting fraud

We have already seen the various areas in which fraud can occur. Fraud can be detected by the experienced manager by simple observation and through experience. Some of the tell-tale and danger signs include:

- employees acting suspiciously – looking shifty and hiding paperwork
- employees with higher levels of spending than you would expect from their income – the payroll clerk who has a new Porsche

- employees working long hours and taking less than the normal holiday entitlement – it is often when employees are away that other employees notice suspicious signs and uncover criminal activity

- employees who have a grudge against the organisation – they may have been passed over for promotion or they may even have a political or ethical axe to grind

- employees who are known to be short of money – they may be struggling with a high mortgage or may even have a drugs problem

### grading likelihood and impact

Part of the process of the management of fraud risk is the decision about whether a risk is a **likely** one or not.  The likelihood of risk can be divided into three levels:

- **high** – the likelihood of fraud is at a high level (disappearing biros)

- **moderate** – the likelihood is possible (theft of cash, collusion)

- **low** – the likelihood is remote (removal of assets from a company pension fund)

The risk of fraud occurring can also be given a **numerical value**: for example a range of 1 to 5, where the higher the risk the higher the number.

Risk assessment also needs to decide whether the **impact** of the fraud is significant. Impact can relate to the **financial state** of the organisation. A major loss through fraud could seriously affect profit and liquidity. For example, the fraudulent trading by an employee of Barings Bank led to its collapse. The fraud can also seriously affect employees, as in the Robert Maxwell case in which employees' pensions were appropriated by the Chairman and Chief Executive.

Generally speaking, frauds that are likely (the disappearing biro) have a lower impact than the remote risk (removal of assets from a company pension fund). The **impact** of a fraud can therefore be similarly graded:

- **high** – the effects of fraud are very serious for the organisation, affecting its profit and/or liquidity

- **moderate** – the effects of the fraud are significant but can be dealt with internally, or in some cases by the police (theft, collusion)

- **low** – the impact of the fraud is insignificant (petty pilfering)

### using a matrix to grade fraud risk

Organisations sometimes use a matrix to assess the extent of fraud risk in an accounting system. The areas of the system in which the fraud might occur must first be identified, for example:

- cash payments
- cash receipts
- sales ledger
- purchases ledger
- expenses
- inventory control
- payroll
- fixed asset purchase

A matrix (or a section of a matrix) will then be drawn up for each of the areas identified. An example of entries in a typical matrix is illustrated below. The matrix might display:

- the identified risk area of the organisation
- the details of the type of fraud
- the role of the employee who may become involved in it
- any third party who may become involved through collusion
- the likelihood of the fraud (high, moderate, low)
- the impact of the fraud (high, moderate, low)

This matrix will then become a valuable tool which will enable management to assess the risks and establish an appropriate strategy for minimising them. Note that the format of the matrices you will encounter in your studies may vary. The example below is fairly typical and could be used in your Report.

### accounting system fraud matrix – some sample entries

| Details of Risk | Employees | Collusion | Likelihood | Impact |
|---|---|---|---|---|
| **Payroll section:**<br>Stationery pilferage | payroll staff | none | high | low |
| Theft of cash | payroll staff | none | moderate | moderate |
| Payments to fictitious employees | payroll staff | third party recipients | moderate | moderate |
| **Purchase ledger:**<br>Paying fictitious suppliers | buyer | third party recipients | moderate | moderate |
| etc . . . etc . . . | | | | |

**Report writing hint**

It is recommended that you should not only research into potential areas of fraud, but you should also identify each type of fraud and grade its **risk** (using a high/medium/low or a numerical system) and its **impact**, using some form of matrix – such as the one on the previous page.

Remember, however, that you will need to be diplomatic with the organisation that you are dealing with, as fraud is a very sensitive issue.

## FRAUD POLICY

Fraud detection is an important function in any internal control system. We have already seen earlier in this chapter some of the warning signs of fraud which managers should look out for as a matter of course. It is useful, however, for an organisation to set up a **Fraud Policy** which might include:

- a clear indication of which managers are responsible for which potential areas of fraud and at what levels

- setting up of control systems to help avoid fraud, eg strict checking, segregation of tasks and division of responsibilities, eg in the purchasing process the person who sets up a purchase order should not be the same as the person who approves it or the person who writes out cheques should not be the same person who signs it (unless maybe it is for a very small amount)

- the regular monitoring of the control systems to ensure that they are working satisfactorily and are amended from time-to-time as circumstances require

- decisions about which type of frauds are significant (eg moderate and high risk) and should be acted upon and those which should be generally guarded against but which are low risk and do not require strict disciplinary action (eg the 'borrowed' biro)

- the need for an anti-fraud 'culture', ie instilling in employees the notion that any form of fraud (including the 'borrowed' biro) is inherently wrong and alerting them to the risks that exist

- following on from the last point, the mechanism should exist for 'whistle-blowing', ie for employees to alert the management if they become aware of any fraudulent goings-on at any level of the organisation; the employee in this case is given protection by the Public Interest Disclosure Act 1998

## action taken to deal with fraud

As part of its Fraud Policy, an organisation should set up a system which ensures that the correct action is taken when:

- fraud is discovered by someone within the organisation
- fraud is reported by someone outside the organisation – the police, for example

Areas which should be dealt with are:

- provision of clear directions to managers about whom to contact when a fraud is discovered
- in a large organisation the appointment of a senior manager with special responsibility for fraud who can take responsibility for any major occurrences
- directions for disciplinary procedures for occurrences of fraud which will not have to involve the police and possible prosecution
- directions for how to deal with a case of fraud which will involve the notification of the police and may result in a criminal prosecution
- directions for how to deal with a case of fraud which is reported to the organisation by the police (eg the discovery of stolen inventory or a bank reporting suspicious money transactions) – and which may result in a criminal prosecution

As you will have gathered from this chapter, fraud is inevitable. The lesson for the organisation is – be prepared.

---

**Report writing hint**

Your report should include a note of any formal Fraud Policy, and if this does not exist, details of managerial control systems and any arrangements made for these systems to be monitored. Evidence of the introduction of any anti-fraud culture could also be included.

---

## some useful websites

www.sfo.gov.uk   www.icaew.com   www.hm-treasury.gov.uk

In order to access information about fraud you are likely to have to carry out a site search on 'fraud'.

This chapter concludes with two Case Studies on fraud and analysis of fraud published by HM Treasury. They should provide you with an understanding of how a weakness in the accounting system can make fraud possible.

# Travel and subsistence fraud

## Case description

This fraud involved an employee who travelled regularly on official business. He **set his own programme** of visits which was **not checked** by his line manager. He then regularly **submitted fraudulent travel and subsistence claims** which included examples of:

- Claiming subsistence allowances **in excess of entitlement;**

- Claiming for overnight stays in hotels when in fact he had **stayed with friends or family;**

- Claiming for **visits not made;**

- **Forging** authorising signatures;

- **Inflating claims** by altering details on claim forms **after authorisation** by countersigning officer.

These claims were paid by the finance team despite the **lack of receipts**, invoices or other supporting documents to verify his expenditure. Travel and subsistence **guidance was also out of date** and consequently had **fallen into disuse**.

The fraud came to light when his office tried to contact him at a hotel where he claimed to be staying. An investigation uncovered a large number of fraudulent claims spanning several years and the officer was eventually prosecuted.

## Control weaknesses

- Inadequate guidance on submitting, authorising and paying claims;

- Inadequate supervision by line management;

- Failure of countersigning officer to verify that journeys had been made;

- Inadequate control exercised by countersigning officer in returning signed claim forms to the claimant rather than passing them directly to the finance team;

- Inadequate checks by finance teams to query amendments to claims, verify countersignatures and ensure that receipts and invoices were included to substantiate claims;

- Absence of spot checks on claims by the finance team management.

# Cash handling fraud

## Case description

Transactions involving receipts of cash or cheques are high risk. Of the cases of staff fraud reported to the Treasury each year, a significant proportion involves misappropriation of cash. In this sample case, a member of staff committed a number of frauds over a period of five years, resulting in a loss of over £10,000.

The organisation's business included the **receipt of cheques** through the post and cash and cheques over the counter. It was the responsibility of the member of staff to receive, record and **prepare the receipts for banking**. She had been in the job several years and her line managers, who trusted her implicitly, had given her **sole responsibility for these duties**. They were no longer carrying out checks or monitoring the process.

She would arrive early each morning, usually before her colleagues, **and open the post on her own**. Money handed in over the counters was also passed to her for banking. However, she **did not record or account for the cheques or money** prior to banking. She would, however, complete a daily cash balance record as part of the **banking reconciliation procedures**, but by this time she had already removed some of the cash and a number of cheques. There were **no independent cross-checks** between the documentation which came with the receipts and the amounts sent for banking. To make matters worse **written procedures were out of date** and had fallen into disuse.

The fraud came to light during the officer's **infrequent absences on leave**. A minor query by a member of the public regarding a previous payment led to an unexplained difference between the amount quoted in the documentation accompanying the payment and the amount recorded by the officer and banked.

Internal audit were brought in to carry out an initial investigation. They identified major discrepancies between records of receipts kept by counter staff, documentation accompanying payments from members of the public and the amounts being banked. The police were called in and under questioning the officer admitted the offences. She had opened a bank account with the initials of the organisation and had been paying in cash and cheques over a five year period. The case was taken to court and on conviction she was given a custodial sentence and had to repay the amounts stolen.

## Control weaknesses

- Lack of separation of duties between post opening, preparation of cash and cheques for banking and reconciliation of amounts banked

- Inadequate supervision and monitoring by line management

- Absence of management checks of accounting records, cash balances or bank reconciliations

- Over-reliance on the honesty and integrity of one individual

- Lack of adequate written instructions

- Unawareness of implications of reluctance to use leave entitlement

- The internal audit report also identified organisational factors which had contributed to the fraud. The main ones were:

  ➢ The organisation had not assessed the risk of fraud;

  ➢ There was no policy statement on fraud;

  ➢ Line managers were not clear about their responsibilities;

  ➢ Manuals and procedures were poorly structured and out of date.

# 4 Reviewing systems and making recommendations

## this chapter covers...

In this chapter we look at the issues involved in reviewing an accounting system and making recommendations for improvement.

The review will involve assessing the strengths of the accounting system:

- seeing how it fulfils the needs of the organisation

- seeing how effective the internal control system is in terms of procedures, communication and training

The review will then assess the weaknesses of the accounting system, analysing

- weaknesses in the internal control system

- the possibilities for error and fraud involving the loss of money, inventory and reputation

The chapter then explains the need to make recommendations for improvement to the accounting system in each area of weakness. This includes analysis of:

- the likely changes needed and the training needs

- the costs involved in each recommendation and the likely benefits that will follow

We look at the way in which these recommendations will impact on the staff involved:

- the help and training that they will need

- the benefits of various computer systems

## WHAT ARE YOU GOING TO REVIEW?

Before you start your review of an accounting system it is important to know exactly what you are going to review. This will depend on a number of factors:

### the method of assessment

You will either be basing your investigation on

- **workplace evidence**, or

- an **AAT Case Study**

If you have chosen to base your assessment on **evidence from an actual workplace**, your choice of area of investigation will largely depend on the size of the organisation. This issue is explained in the next section.

If you chose an **AAT Case Study**, the choice of the area to investigate is made for you. The sample AAT assessment at the back of this book, for example (see page 81) is based on a small business. It sets out a defined scenario and the task is made easier for you in that the description of what is going on in the accounting system – including all its many problems and shortcomings – are set out for you to analyse and make recommendations.

### the size of the organisation

If the organisation is large, say a large company or public sector organisation, the accounting system may also be large and highly departmentalised. To review the whole system will be an immense task and you would be well advised to chose just a part of it, payroll for example. As your investigation will then be limited in breadth, you will need to research in greater depth.

If, on the other hand, the organisation is smaller, a family business for example, you are likely to need to take a wider view of the accounting system. It is very possible that the system in this case is operated by a limited number of people who each take on a number of the various accounting functions such as payroll, sales ledger and cashiering. In this situation your review is likely to cover more of the accounting roles.

The main functional areas required for an accounting system have already been mentioned in Chapter 2. They include:

- the individual ledgers: purchases ledger, sales ledger and nominal ledger
- credit control
- cash handling and banking

- petty cash
- payroll
- budgeting and management reporting

If you choose the accounting system of a large organisation to review, you could restrict your investigation to one of these areas. If you are dealing with a small organisation which has a simple structure you could evaluate a larger number of areas.

### review method

We will now look at the method you should adopt when reviewing an accounting system. Basically this involves analysing:

- the **strengths** of the existing system – in terms of its internal control system, cost-effectiveness, reliability and speed
- the **weaknesses** of the existing system – they will form the reasoning for the recommendations for improvement that you will make

## IDENTIFYING THE STRENGTHS OF THE SYSTEM

There are various areas of investigation which will indicate how well established the accounting system is and how effective it is in preventing errors and deterring fraud.

As a first step you could:

- draw up an organisational chart of the accounting system showing the areas of responsibility and the various reporting lines
- identify the other operational areas of the organisation which it supports

You can then investigate in more detail the internal control system to see how reliable it is. You can ask questions which relate to a number of different aspects of internal control:

### operating procedures?

*'Is there a Policies and Procedures (or similar) document*

*'Is the authorisation system for payments clear and workable?'*

*'Are there the necessary routine checking procedures in place?'*

*'Are there random checks made to ensure procedures are being followed correctly?'*

*'Are the records kept in an organised way and is confidentiality respected as appropriate?'*

*'Are passwords (both to computers and premises) kept secure and changed when necessary?'*

*'Are items such as the petty cash box and the company cheque books kept under lock and key and are the keys kept only by authorised staff?*

*'Are the reporting lines within the accounting system clearly defined?'*

*'Are the reporting lines with other parts of the organisation working efficiently?'*

*'Is the system cost-effective – does it use resources efficiently?'*

## reliability and speed?

Questions include:

*'Is the system completely reliable, eg if staff are away?'*

*' Does the system  operate efficiently and without unnecessary delays?'*

## computer systems?

A well-organised accounting system should ideally have an integrated computer system on a network using proprietory software such as Sage and Microsoft Office. This will enable accounting staff to input and access their own accounting data and also have access to other data kept in the system – subject to passwords and authorisation, of course.

A well-developed computer system will also help when new or temporary staff are brought in and have to get used to the organisation's routine and procedures at short notice

## staff training?

An effective accounting system will operate well if the staff are well-trained in a range of processes and are multi-skilled. This is especially true of a small business where staff have to cover for colleagues who are off sick, on holiday, or on maternity leave. As we will see later in this chapter, training comes at a cost and will need to be able to repay the investment.

> **Report writing hint**
>
> When you are investigating the strength of an internal control system, make sure you look at and assess all relevant areas: operating procedures, communications, cost-effectiveness, reliability, speed of operation, computer systems, and staff training.

All these aspects of a well-developed accounting system contribute to its **strength**. It is when the system fails in some or all of these areas that **weaknesses** appear and errors and fraud can then occur.

## IDENTIFYING THE WEAKNESSES OF THE SYSTEM

The weaknesses in an accounting system often result in **errors** or in **fraud**.

### errors

**Errors** result from inefficiencies in the internal control system and can cause all sorts of problems, for example:

- an invoice being sent to the wrong customer
- a discount being incorrectly calculated
- a payment to a supplier being made very late
- an employee being paid the wrong rate of pay
- a customer being sent a formal demand for an overdue account when in fact payment has already been received but entered to the wrong account

You will doubtless be able to add other examples to this list of unfortunate accidents. What these examples have in common is that they result in some form of loss to the organisation involved:

- **loss of money** – when a payment is made for the wrong amount or a discount is incorrectly calculated
- **loss of time** – when a problem has to be sorted out and emails and apologies sent – time is also money, of course
- **loss of reputation** – when customer expectations are not met and the organisation loses face – and even its customer's business

### fraud

**Fraud**, which was covered in detail in the last chapter, is another consequence of basic weaknesses in the internal control system of an organisation. It also poses a threat of loss:

- **loss of money** – monetary-based frauds include purchase ledger staff paying fictitious suppliers and diverting the money to their own account, or payroll staff using the same principle to send payroll payments to fictitious employees
- **loss of inventory** – for example, a case of an employee over-ordering valuable inventory and then stealing it and arranging for its sale at a nearby street market
- **loss of time** – employees overstating time worked on time sheets

It is probably unlikely that you will uncover any major frauds when basing your assessment on workplace evidence, but you should write about the possible causes of fraud and the ways in which fraud can be prevented.

> **Report writing hint**
>
> When you are investigating the weaknesses of an internal control system, and the ways in which they will make errors or fraud possible, assess the weaknesses in terms of the way in which the organisation will lose out – whether it relates to money, inventory, time or reputation.

## practical examples of weaknesses

The AAT Case Study route to assessment will inevitably provide situations which illustrate weaknesses in an accounting system.

The examples of situations quoted below are taken from the Sample Case Study at the back of this book. Suggestions are made on the next page for the weaknesses they expose in the internal control system of the accounting function.

---

### security codes

Access to the accounts office is gained through a keypad code, the code for which is UOYAB (Bayou – the boss's name – read backwards). This code is relatively common knowledge throughout the company as it is also the alarm code for the building, and is used by the warehouse store supervisors and manager when they close up in the evenings.

When the computer system was set-up a password was installed to protect the work. This is also UOYAB, as John uses the same security code for everything throughout the company because he feels this makes life easier.

### cash and banking

Banking is carried out on a Monday and Thursday, and this is normally Gary's job which he does during his lunch break. The Thursday banking of cash is often lower as John has now started to reduce the cheques drawn for wages by the amount of cash available in the office safe on a Thursday morning. His idea is that any cash available can be used to supplement the making up of the wages to reduce the amount of cash needed to be drawn from the bank. There is no petty cash system as such. If cash is needed for any incidental expenses, this is taken from the till floats and a note put in the till to cover this.

### payroll

Jo had booked two weeks holiday over Christmas, as she wanted to spend this time with Harry. As she knew that she is the only member of staff who can operate the Sage payroll system she decided to complete three weeks pay packets on the same date – all based on the hours worked in the current week. She completed the pay packets and placed them in the safe, informing the supervisors that Gary will give them out on the correct Friday and that any over or under payments will be adjusted during the following week after she has returned to work.

**POSSIBLE WEAKNESSES IN THE ACCOUNTING SYSTEM** (see the situations on the previous page)

### security codes

The password system in this organisations is very lax:

1    The password is easily worked out and remembered because it is the boss's name spelt backwards.

2    The same password is used for a variety of different purposes.

3    There is no indication that the password is ever changed.

4    There is open opportunity for fraud: the code is used for the warehouse store by the supervisors and manager when they lock up. Theft of inventory is easily possible.

### cash and banking

The accounting system's arrangements for cash handling and recording of cash payments seems to be non-existent:

1    There is no petty cash system.

2    There appears to be no checking system for cash counting.

3    Cash is passed from the tills to the safe to the payroll assistant with no record of any kind being made of the transactions.

4    No accounting entries appear to reflect the movements in cash.

5    There is an open invitation to theft.

### payroll

The payroll system has a number of weaknesses:

1    Only one person in the organisation is trained to operate Sage payroll.

2    Working out wages by guesswork without using timesheets is unacceptable practice.

3    To estimate future wage packets on one week's figures is also unacceptable practice.

4    There is apparently no consideration given to the PAYE implications of these estimates and potential amendments.

## MAKING THE RECOMMENDATIONS

The review of the organisation's accounting system will have revealed:

- the **strengths** of its internal control system and the way in which it operates
- the **weaknesses** of the system and the consequent errors that occur and opportunities for fraud that exist

Whether you are basing your Report on workplace evidence or on the AAT Case Study you will now need to:

- make recommendations for improvement
- justify those recommendations

As noted earlier in this chapter, if you are dealing with a **large organisation** you may have restricted your investigation to a single area and found a single area of weakness, for example the need to computerise a manual system. If this is the case you should be making two or three separate recommendations for improvement – eg various different computer system solutions – and weighing up the advantages and disadvantages of each.

If on the other hand you have investigated a **small organisation**, you are likely to be taking an overview of the whole accounting system and you will probably have identified and assessed a number of areas for improvement. In this case you should be providing a recommendation for each weakness.

> **Report writing hint**
>
> When you are investigating the weaknesses of an internal control system, make sure that what you are taking on is realistic. If you have identified a number of weaknesses (if it is a small business, for example) you should provide a recommendation for each one. If you are concentrating on a single area of weakness (eg inventory control in a large warehouse) you should provide a number of recommendations (eg different inventory control systems), comparing them for their advantages and disadvantages.

### the importance of the computer system

One aspect of your review and recommendations is the importance of the computer system. It may be that the accounting system uses a variety of different computers which are standalone machines, possibly with different operating systems, using different software for the same purpose. It is possible that the accounting system only uses computers for some of the accounting functions, for example invoicing but not for payroll. It is even possible that the accounting system does not use computers at all!

The ideal set-up is likely to be a system:

- that uses similar or identical computers, all with the same operating system
- linked on a network
- using the same software (loaded with the same version), eg Sage for accounting transactions and payroll, and Microsoft Office (Word, Excel, Access) for processing text, spreadsheets and database records

A further  example taken from the AAT sample Case Study assessment reproduced at the end of this book is a typical example of an accounting system that is deficient in this respect and obviously needs bringing up-to-date:

---

**computers**

These are all run on a stand-alone basis, though they are all linked to the same printer.

Gary has designed a form in Microsoft Office Word which he uses as a pro forma for invoicing.

Gary allows two half days per month for the task of telephoning customers who are late in paying; drawing the information from an aged debtors control listing which has been set up on the Excel system to indicate customers whose accounts are outstanding for more than sixty days.

Jo had booked two weeks holiday over Christmas, as she wanted to spend this time with Harry (her son). As she knew that she is the only member of staff who can operate the Sage payroll system she decided to complete three weeks pay packets on the same date – all based on the hours worked in the current week.

---

There are **many weaknesses** in the computer system of this business:

- the computers are stand-alone and so cannot link up with each other for data interchange
- invoicing is carried out on a Word pro forma rather than on a dedicated computer accounting program
- the Aged Debtors Schedule is drawn up on Excel, which means all the figures need to be entered manually – a very time-consuming operation
- only one employee knows how to use Sage Payroll which leads to some very unconventional accounting practices!

In your **recommendations for improvement** you could suggest that a new computer system could be established with the following features:

- a network of computers using the same software, possibly Microsoft Office (or a suitable alternative)

- the acquisition of a Sage accounting package (eg Sage 50, or a suitable alternative) which will be able to:

  - integrate with Sage Payroll

  - handle the invoicing

  - deal with the Nominal, Sales and Purchase ledgers

  - produce an Aged Debtors Schedule (or be configured to export data to Excel)

  - invest in staff training for the staff in Sage and Microsoft Office so that things do not grind to a halt when staff are away

## impact on the staff

A new or updated computer system or any significant change in the accounting system will clearly impact on the staff involved. They will feel challenged, and perhaps threatened.

Part of any recommendation for change should include a plan for ensuring that the staff will acquire the necessary skills and knowledge so that they can use the revised system effectively. This could include:

- internal training courses

- external training courses

- 'teach-yourself' facilities such as manuals, DVDs, online tutorials and the 'Help' menus provided with the computer software

- telephone support lines made available by the software provider (Sage, for example, provide an excellent 'helpline')

Staff training can be an expensive item and should form a prominent element in the cost-benefit analysis (see below) which assesses the total costs of a recommendation against the benefits provided.

Not all recommendations for improvement of the accounting system will necessarily involve computers. Recommendations may include other modifications to the internal control system which will impact on staff because they will change everyday working processes. For example

- improvements to checking procedures, eg supplier invoices paid

- improvements to authorisation procedures, eg sending of BACS payments to suppliers

- increased security of cash handling, eg having two people to check tills

- increased password security, eg changing passwords regularly

All of these changes would need to be communicated to staff, incorporated in the operating instructions (Procedures) of the accounting system, and monitored on a regular basis. This too will cost money.

## HOW MUCH WILL IT ALL COST? – COST-BENEFIT ANALYSIS

**Cost-benefit analysis** compares the amount of resources used (which are measured in money terms) with the benefits obtained from a project (which are not always measurable in money terms).

### what are the costs?

Cost-benefit analysis involves analysing and quantifying the potential costs of implementing an improvement in the accounting system. For example, there may be extra costs incurred in employing more staff, in staff training and acquiring new computer systems.

On the 'benefit' side you will need to analyse the benefits from a project that cannot be measured in financial terms, for example:

• better communication links between staff

• an improvement in the quality of a service provided to clients/customers

• a more effective reporting system

Cost-benefit analysis tells you whether the benefits will outweigh the costs.

### cost-benefit analysis – a practical example

**Installation of a new computer system in the Accounts Department**

An estimate of the likely costs is as follows:

|  | £ |
|---|---|
| – the cost of the hardware | 50,000 |
| – the cost of the software | 10,000 |
| – the installation cost | 2,500 |
| – the cost of training the staff | 3,790 |
| – annual maintenance cost | 1,750 |
| – insurance of hardware and for loss of data | 1,250 |
| | 69,290 |

When working out a statement of costs you should show how you arrived at the **training costs**. These costs include the cost of the time spent training by the employees of the organisation which would otherwise have been spent in productive work. A typical calculation might look like this:

| time spent by a manager in training | £ |
|---|---|
| 20 hours x £50 per hour | 1,000 |
| plus 15% on employer costs | |
| (National Insurance etc) | 150 |
| **time spent by 8 assistants in training** | |
| 20 hours  x  8  x  £10 per hour | 1,600 |
| plus 15% on employer costs | |
| (National Insurance etc) | 240 |
| **time spent by external trainer** | |
| 20 hours  x  £40 per hour | 800 |
| **TOTAL TRAINING COST** | 3,790 |

## assessing the benefits

You may well ask 'What is the cost of the benefits?'

Sometimes the benefit will result in a monetary advantage, although this is difficult to quantify and would not be expected in your recommendations

A new computerised system means that money savings can be made in the way the system operates, for example:

- many routine operations will be speeded up which will save time and therefore reduce the wages bill

- electronic statements of account to customers will save on postage

- electronic payments to suppliers will also save time and money

- computer printed invoices will have fewer errors and therefore save time and money

There are also benefits which cannot be quantified in terms of money:

- the organisation will appear more professional

- the service provided by the organisation will be more efficient, which means that there will be fewer errors and problems, all of which cost time and money

## conclusion

In conclusion, you will see that the benefits provided by a cost-benefit analysis cannot always be given a monetary value. The final decision must rest on the evidence of all the benefits provided – in basic terms "will it significantly improve the accounting system and is it worth all the money?"

**Report writing hint**

When you make a recommendation for an improvement in an accounting system you should always carry out a cost-benefit analysis, giving a monetary value to the costs wherever possible.

If you cannot work out an exact cost an approximation is better than not quoting a cost at all.

## inspiration page – for your notes

# 5 Writing the Report

*This chapter offers practical advice on the writing of the Report. It covers:*

- *the context of the Report in the assessment process*

- *the structure of the Report – the sections that it contains*

- *the writing process – keeping to 3,500 - 4,000 words*

- *the writing style to be used*

- *the contents of the various sections of the Report*

- *establishing a plan and a time schedule for the Report*

- *the individual responsibilities of the student, assessor and workplace mentor (if the Report is based on a real workplace)*

## THE REPORT AND THE ASSESSMENT PROCESS

The 3,500 - 4,000 word Report is the main part of the assessment of the 'Internal Control and Accounting Systems' Learning Area.

If you base your Report on workplace evidence, as opposed to the the AAT Case Study, you need:

- a signed declaration from your employer – an '**employer testimony**' ('letter of authenticity') which confirms that the Report is your own original work and aims to improve the quality and management of the accounting system; if you are not in employment, the testimony should be signed by the manager of the workplace you have investigated

- answers to further **questioning** to cover any assessment criteria (see Chapter 1) not covered in the Report or in its appendices

The Report is therefore at the core of the assessment and you will make life much easier for yourself if you provide as much as you can in the Report.

Your assessor is likely to provide some form of checklist or mapping document so that you can record and cross reference the required assessment criteria by paragraph number as it is produced in the writing of the Report.

## STRUCTURE OF THE REPORT – AN OVERVIEW

The Report should normally be presented in standard **report format**. A summary of a recommended format is shown on the next page. It is adapted and expanded from a template produced by the AAT.

Report headings, such as the ones shown on the summary, may vary according to the format adopted and from organisation to organisation, but the critical point is that all the elements of a standard report should be present. It should be a closely argued document; if anything is left out, it will fail to communicate its findings and conclusions effectively.

We will cover the required writing style in detail later in this chapter. All you need to appreciate at this point is that a report is a formal document and not a personal diary. It should be formal in structure, in page layout and in its language.

## SUGGESTED REPORT CONTENTS

**title page**
a statement of what the Report is about, quoting your student name and membership number

**list of contents (index)**
a full list of all the Report sections with page references

**terms of reference**
why the Report is being written – to cover the Learning Area 'Internal Control and Accounting Systems' and also to recommend improvements to an accounting system

**executive summary**
a short summary of the Report (stressing its conclusions) designed to be read by the management of the organisation concerned

**methodology**
how you planned and went about compiling the information for the Report, acknowledging and thanking the people who helped you

**organisation background**
a factual summary of what the organisation does, its products, customers, suppliers and stakeholders

**analysis and evaluation**
an analysis of the strengths and weaknesses of the current accounting system and how they affect the organisation, plus an identification of areas where errors and fraud could occur

**recommendations**
possible solutions to the area(s) of weakness, setting out the choice of the preferred course of action and an implementation plan

**cost benefit analysis**
an assessment of the quantifiable cost of the proposed changes in relation to the qualitative benefits of the changes – this could form part of the 'recommendations' section

**appendices**
extra material such as organisation charts, questionnaires and other supporting documents

**letter of authenticity**
a letter from the workplace manager confirming that you personally have carried out the work in the Report

**mapping**
cross referencing to the assessment requirements of the Report by paragraph number

## HINTS ON THE WRITING PROCESS

### what is 3,500 - 4000 words?

The upper limit of your Report is 4,000 words. You will be relieved to hear that this does not require a very long report. A normal full page might contain 500 words on average, so 4,000 words will fill eight pages of normal word-processed text. You should aim for the equivalent of between seven and eight pages. Note that the final Report may be longer because each section starts on a new page. The 4,000 word limit does not include the appendices, so you are free to include as much supporting material as you need, but it must be relevant and you must take care to avoid any breaches of confidentiality if you include copies of internal documents and accounting data.

### word-processed format

The Report should be produced on the computer mainly because it has to be submitted online. Word-processing programs will also enable you to carry out editing, produce tables and also make regular spellchecks and word counts. Also note that:

* the sections (eg 'Terms of Reference' and 'Methodology') should all start on a new page
* the sections and the paragraphs should be numbered; eg if 'Methodology' is Section 4, the paragraphs in that Section will be numbered 4.1, 4.2, 4.3, and so on.

### writing style

A formal report requires straightforward written English. There is nothing particularly difficult about producing written English; the problems lie with the current tendency to write as you speak, or as you text, or as you email. The result is often an abbreviated form of written English which as you will appreci8 does nt work 2 well on the page.

Another problem facing people who are not used to writing formal written English is that they think of it as some sort of overblown 'posh' sounding language which has to be complicated and impressive to make its point. Nothing could be further from the truth. The test of good written English is that it should be:

* plain and simple
* to the point
* understandable by a twelve year-old

You might think that the last point is some form of a joke, but you might be surprised to learn that quality newspapers aim for this level of reading ability. To sum up, the first rule of writing is 'keep it simple'. Good writing must be clear. Use short sentences. Get the message across.

## hints on writing plain English in a report

* use **simple words** instead of complicated ones

* use **short sentences** instead of long ones

* use the **active tense** rather than the passive, eg 'the line manager *carries out* regular checks on the petty cash book' rather than 'regular checks *are carried out* on the petty cash book by the line manager'

* use the **third person** (he, she, they) rather than 'I' or 'we' – remember that the Report should be a formal analysis rather than 'this is what I think about . . .'

* **avoid slang** eg 'the line manager really *hacked off* the rest of the staff'; you should use the word 'annoyed' instead of 'hacked' to avoid the innocent reader assuming that some form of serious injury had taken place

* avoid **abbreviations** such as 'isn't', didn't' and write the phrases in full: 'is not' and 'did not'

* avoid **jargon** and **acronyms** which may not be understood by the general reader, for example 'the FD disapproved of the BOGOF policy because it reduced margins' which means 'the Finance Director disapproved of the 'buy one, get one free' policy because it reduced margins'

## other practical report writing hints

You may find that you will end up cutting material to keep within the limit. Remember that the important material is your analysis of the accounting system and your recommendations for change. If you need to make cuts, they should be from the introductory sections which describe the organisation, its products, customers, suppliers and stakeholders.

Remember to back-up your work each time you work on your Report. There are too many sad stories such as 'I did my Report on my lap-top, but the hard disk corrupted and I lost the lot.'

Read what you have written. Print out copies of what you have done as you go along so that you can check your work.

Ask other people to read what you have written to make sure that the reader can understand your meaning. Your workplace mentor and assessor will obviously read what you write, but it is useful to ask a friend or a partner as well, as long as you do not endanger a serious relationship in the process.

## SECTIONS OF THE REPORT

On the next few pages we will illustrate the various sections of the Report, all of which should start on a new page. We will explain what the headings mean and give an idea of what should be included in each section.

Remember that report headings and formats are likely to vary from one organisation to another. The format shown here is often used, although the same basic structure should be common to any report. You should adopt the format you are used to, or, if you are not familiar with any format, you would be advised to adopt the format illustrated here.

### title page

The title page should state:

- what the Report is about
- the purpose of the Report
- your name
- your AAT student membership number
- the date of submission

The title should *not* be 'Internal Control and Accounting Systems'.

An example is shown below.

---

**An analysis of the manual accounting operations of Didgeree Limited with recommendations for conversion to a Sage 50 computer accounting system.**

Submitted by: A S Tudent

AAT student membership number: N001999

Date: March 2011

This Report is submitted for assessment of the AAT Learning and Assessment Area 'Internal Control and Accounting Systems.'

---

## list of contents

The list of contents should list each section, including the appendices, in page order and give accurate page references.

Note that every section should start on a new page. This will mean, of course, that the Report will run to more than the number of pages that 3,500 to 4,000 words will normally fill as solid text.

---

**List of Contents**

| | page |
|---|---|
| Terms of reference | 1 |
| Executive summary | 2 |
| Methodology | 3 |
| Background to Didgeree Limited | 4 |
| The accounting function of Didgeree Limited | 6 |

. . . and so on

---

## terms of reference

The terms of reference outline the **reasons for writing the Report**. These are:

- why the Report is required – ie it is part of your AAT assessment
- the objectives of the Report set out by AAT – ie what you are hoping to achieve in the Report

Note the use of paragraph numbering and bullet points to clarify the text.

---

**1 Terms of Reference**

1.1 This Report has been prepared to cover the assessment requirements of AAT Learning and Assessment Area 'Internal Control and Accounting Systems.'

1.2 The objectives of this Report are to:

- analyse the manual accounting system of Didgeree Limited in order to identify areas of weakness
- make recommendations for improving the accounting system through the introduction of a computerised system

## executive summary

This is likely to be one of the last sections that you write. It is a report summary written for the senior (executive) management of the organisation involved. The object of the summary is to set out in a nutshell:

- the analysis that took place – eg of a manual accounting system

- the changes recommended to be made to the accounting system – eg through the computerisation of various sections of the accounting system, using Sage 50

- a conclusion analysing the impact of the changes on the organisation – the benefits (speed, accuracy, better and up-to-date management information) outweighing the costs (hardware, software, training)

This summary need be no more than a page of text, presented in succinct paragraphs. Remember that the management reading the summary will be very familiar with the organisation (they manage it, after all) and will also be short of time!

## methodology

This section is also sometimes headed 'Procedures'. It briefly describes the research methods used in producing the Report. This section should include:

- a brief description of the way in which you analysed the accounting system and consulted with the people managing it and working within it, eg by observation, monitoring, questionnaire, interview

- details of any people from outside the organisation that you used as an information source, eg customers, computer consultants

- use of any 'written' sources, eg books, manuals, websites (note that you should not list them here, but include details in an appendix)

It is normal and polite practice to acknowledge and thank in this section all the people you have consulted.

## organisation background

This section is often the first part of the Report that you will write as it is easy to put together and will get rid of the blank sheet of paper syndrome.

What is required here is a brief description of the organisation which is the subject of your Report. Details you could include are:

- its name and location

- legal status (eg limited company, local authority department, charity)

- how long it has been functioning

- what it does: its main 'products' and 'markets'

- its customers
- main competitors
- its stakeholders (ie others who may have an interest of some kind in the organisation), eg the public, regulatory authorities, pressure groups
- structure of the organisation – where the accounting function fits in (you could include an organisation chart in the appendices)

Remember that this section is intended to 'set the scene' and should not be overburdened with too much detail. Remember also that the Report is a report to management, and they will presumably know about most of what you include in this section. Clear paragraph numbering will help in this section, for example . . .

---

### 4   Organisation background

4.1   Didgeree Limited is a limited company, established in 1985 in Milburn, West Midlands.

4.2   Its main business is the importation and marketing of Australian giftware through its 'Boomerang' wholesale and mail order operations. Its customers are UK retail stores and mail order buyers. It has no significant UK competitor.

4.3   Its main stakeholders are the import regulatory authorities and environmental pressure groups who have objected to the sale of goods made from possum skins.

4.4   Didgeree Limited is organised into departments (including Accounting Department) – see Appendix 5 on page 22 for a structure chart.

---

### analysis and evaluation of the current system

This section should start with a brief description of the workings of the Accounting Department. Again, a structure chart can be included in the Appendices. The details might include:

- the different sections of the Department, eg Purchases Ledger, Sales Ledger, Payroll and the approximate number of people employed
- where you fit into the Department (if you work in it)

But the important part of this section is your **analysis** of the Accounting Department and the highlighting of weaknesses.

A useful starting point for this analysis is the SWOT approach. 'SWOT' is a traditional management analytical technique. The letters stand for the identification of **s**trengths, **w**eaknesses, **o**pportunities and **t**hreats.

**S**trengths      These are the 'plus' points of the accounting system and its management – for example an integrated computer accounting system which saves time and money, an efficient checking procedure or well trained staff.

**W**eaknesses      These are the areas that you will need to identify in order to carry out improvements to the accounting system. These weaknesses could be identified in a manual accounting system and also in a computerised accounting system. They might include, for example, lack of training and insufficient staffing or previous generation computer hardware which is incompatible with new software. They might open up the possibility of errors and fraud.

**O**pportunities      These are areas of an organisation (the accounting system in this case) which could be improved and developed and become the 'strengths', the 'plus' points. For example a manual accounting system could be computerised.

**T**hreats      Threats are external to the accounting system and could include possible outsourcing of accounting activities or a merger with another organisation.

**Note:** a SWOT analysis is a useful document for focusing your ideas on the strengths and weaknesses of an accounting system but it is lengthy and, if you do one, **it must be included as an Appendix to your Report**.

Your **findings** should follow on from your analysis of the present accounting system and identification of weaknesses. They could include the results of any employee questionnaire(s). Completed questionnaire sheets could be included in an Appendix.

## recommendations and cost benefit analysis

This section will set out what you think are the causes of the problem(s), suggest possible solutions and choose a preferred option with the help of a cost benefit analysis. This should weigh up the costs (eg new computers and training) and show the benefits (long-term efficiencies). **Remember that every weakness identified should have at least one recommendation for improvement.**

## appendices

Appendices:

- are not included in the final word count

- should be numbered

- should be cross-referenced where appropriate in the text

- should be relevant to the subject matter of the Report

- may include confidential material and so it is essential that the permission of the relevant organisation is given before material can be used

Examples of appendices include:

- structure charts of the organisation and its accounting system

- relevant financial documents, eg sample invoices

- SWOT analysis

- internal memoranda and minutes of meetings

- budgets

- questionnaires used and analyses of findings from the questionnaires

As noted above, the appendices should be relevant and refer to the text of the Report.

Avoid the temptation to use the appendices as a dumping ground for excess material.

The appendices are excluded from the Report word count.

## and do not forget . . . your letter of authenticity

If the Report is based on a real workplace you will need a letter from your workplace manager – an employer testimony – to authenticate your Report; it should state that:

- the Report is all your own work

- the confidentiality aspects have been covered

The letter must be:

- on headed paper and dated

- signed by the workplace manager, with his/her name and job title

An example letter of authenticity is shown at the top of the next page.

**Didgeree Limited**
Unit 3 Bush Industrial Estate
Ramsay Road
Milburn
WM6 5FG

Tel 01901 456271 Fax 01901 457829

J H Potter
Department of Professional Studies
Milburn College of Technology
Forest Road
Milburn
WM3 6RA

1 April 2011

Dear Mr Potter

Accounting Systems Report

This is to testify that Jos Cobber is a Finance Assistant in the Accounting Department at Didgeree Limited.

Jos Cobber has undertaken this Report, during the performance of her work, with the aim of improving the quality and management of the accounting system of the company.

This confirms that the Report is Jos Cobber's original work and that she has the permission of Didgeree Limited to reproduce the data contained in the body of the Report and in the appendices.

Yours sincerely

*J Kennedy*

J Kennedy, Accounts Manager

## mapping

An important document related to the completion of your assessment is the **mapping** carried out by you and your assessor to make sure that all the assessment criteria have been covered, either in the Report itself or by giving answers to additional questions provided by your assessor. You should ask your assessor about this requirement.

**Mapping** involves cross referencing in a formal checklist all the Learning and Assessment Area assessment criteria. See Chapter 1 (pages 12 and 13) for the assessment criteria.

## TIME PLANNING

In the first chapter of this book we illustrated the processes needed for the successful completion of your Report, using the diagram reproduced on the next page.

Efficient **time planning** is essential so that you can get going as soon as possible. You should be guided by your own training provider who will have planned a timetable for you, whether you use workplace evidence or the AAT Case Study for your evidence. We explain the process for both below.

### timetable for Report based on workplace evidence

Stage 1    **Decide on your subject** – in discussion with your assessor and workplace mentor.

During this period you should be **studying the theoretical areas** of organisations, accounting systems, internal control systems and fraud, covering all the required assessment criteria. You should at the same time be planning the Report. You could make a start on the Report and write **the first 500 words** for submission to your assessor – this could be the description of the organisation you have chosen for the Report.

Stage 2    During the second stage you should **complete the first draft** of the complete Report, suitably mapped to the assessment criteria, so that it can be sent online to your assessor. You are then likely to have a series of **assessor interviews** to finalise the Report. If you find that there are assessment criteria that still need covering you will at this stage be able to provide additional evidence through extra questioning in the form of a Word file, a pdf or even a video file. This can then be submitted to AAT electronically.

### timetable for Report based on an AAT Case Study

Stage 1    As you will not have to worry about choosing a workplace, you should use this period of time to **study the theoretical areas** of organisations, accounting systems, internal control systems and fraud, covering all the required assessment criteria, under the direction of your assessor. You should also make yourself familiar with the **report format**.

Stage 2    You will be given the AAT Case Study and will have four months to complete and submit your Report to AAT, using the evidence in the Case Study and your assessor to help you.

## suggested assessment plan – using workplace evidence

**choosing workplace**
or other organisation
to assess
as the basis of the Report

**choosing subject area(s)**
within the accounting system
- evaluating system
- planning and evaluating possible
changes to the accounting system

**using experience**
- in workplace
or
- situations described in
AAT Case Study

**AGREE SUBJECT
WITH ASSESSOR**

**consulting with people**
- workplace mentor
or manager
- training assessor
- timescale
- content
- resources needed

**THE FIRST 500
WORDS**

**learning from this book**
- about the format and
style of the Report

- about what you need to
include in the Report

- the theory of
organisations, accounting
systems, internal control
and fraud

**DRAFT REPORT
COMPLETED**

**mapping**
checking that the
Report covers the
assessment criteria

**assessor interviews**

**FINAL REPORT
SUBMISSION**

**producing extra
evidence**
to cover the assessment
criteria not covered in
the Report

## RESPONSIBILITIES FOR THE REPORT

Although it is the student who has to write the Report, it is important to appreciate that the responsibilities for its successful completion are shared with the assessor and the workplace mentor/manager. The responsibilities for the Report are summarised below.

### student responsibilities

Some teaching centres recommend that the student draws up a formal assessment plan setting out the various tasks and deadlines as agreed with the assessor. This plan is then signed by the student. A possible format is . . .

---

**ASSESSMENT PLAN**

| Task | Planned completion date | Actual completion date |
|------|------------------------|------------------------|
|      |                        |                        |
|      |                        |                        |

**I confirm I have agreed to the planned completion dates and will do my best to meet them.**

signed  ----------------------------------------------------------------

name  ----------------------------------------------------------------

date  ----------------------------------------------------------------

---

Tasks that could be listed in this plan include:

- choose the subject for the Report
- choose a workplace mentor
- write the first 500 words
- complete research
- complete first draft
- map content against assessment criteria
- preliminary assessor interview

- produce any extra evidence required
- final assessor interview

Further responsibilities of the student include:

- meeting with the assessor at agreed times
- liaising with the workplace mentor/manager when necessary
- ensuring that any confidentiality issues have been sorted out

## assessor responsibilities

The assessor's overall responsibility is to guide the student through the assessment process to a successful completion of the Report and the required evidence. Specific responsibilities to each student include:

- planning a realistic  assessment programme
- agreeing the subject of the Report through one-to-one sessions with the student
- monitoring the production of evidence and ensuring that it is the student's own work
- checking the evidence against the requirements
- carrying out a preliminary assessment interview based on the Report first draft
- providing any additional assessment requirements that may be necessary to ensure that all the assessment criteria have been covered
- assessing the Report final version
- carrying out the final assessment interview

## workplace mentor responsibilities

The workplace mentor – who may be your boss or a senior employee in the area you are investigating – fulfils an important role in helping you complete your Report. This person should:

- help you initially identify the workplace problems which you will try to remedy through the recommendations in your Report
- help you to obtain the evidence you need
- if possible, read through what you have written
- resolve any problems of confidentiality of information
- authenticate your work (see page 75 for a sample authentication letter)

### Report writing hints

1 Ensure that you have identified a suitable format for your Report. This can be a format used by your own organisation, or you can adopt the format shown in this chapter (see page 66).

2 Make sure that you know in your own mind what the maximum of 4,000 words represents.

3 Ensure that you have access to a suitable word-processing package, that you can print out drafts of your work, email them to your assessor, and, very importantly, that you can back-up your work.

4 Construct a time plan or an assessment plan. Make sure that your deadlines are firmly in your mind.

5 Remember to start each new section on a new page.

6 Read through your own work regularly and ask yourself 'Is this written in simple English? Can it be easily understood?'

7 Ask other people to read through your own work and ask them the same questions: 'Is this written in simple English? Can it be easily understood?'

8 As you write your report ensure that you are referencing it, as you go along, to the assessment criteria in the format suggested by your tutor.

9 Organise your appendices efficiently. Make references to them in the text where appropriate. Only include relevant material.

10 Arrange to party when you have completed your Report.

# AAT Sample Case Study Assessment

## Internal control and accounting systems

This Sample Case Study has been produced by the Association of Accounting Technicians and is reproduced here with their kind permission. The sample Case Study starts on page 82 and the questions to be answered start on page 89.

# BAYOU STORES LIMITED

*This sample case study is intended to indicate the type of situation that candidates will be presented with, and as such should be considered as an abridged version of those that will actually be used for live assessments.*

## INTRODUCTION TO THE BUSINESS AND THE OWNER

Bayou Stores Ltd. is a large wholesale warehouse supplying a range of groceries, cleaning materials and other household goods to small, independent grocery stores.

It was set up in 2008 by John Bayou, who having taken early retirement from his job as a fire fighter, used his pension and an inheritance to set up the business on the edge of Grantchester, a large industrial city. Besides the warehouse, John, who is single, has only one hobby, which is golf. He usually spends all day Friday at the golf club – and, other than this, he works very long hours for the other six days a week.

He employs 30 staff in the stores and three part-time staff in the small accounts department. You have just been employed to work as the senior accounts clerk and, as the only full-time staff member, to supervise the running of the office.

The store is open seven days a week, and operates from 7am until 10pm, Monday to Friday and from 10am to 6pm on Saturday and Sunday, whilst the accounts department only opens from 9am until 5pm Monday to Friday.

### The Accounts Department

The accounts department's office is located on the first floor, over the warehouse store, which occupies the whole of the ground floor of the building. Access to the office is by stairs or an elevator from the ground floor – and this access is often used by the public – as the toilet facilities for staff and customers are also located on the first floor. Once on this floor access to the accounts office is gained through a keypad code, the code for which is UOYAB (Bayou read backwards). This code is relatively common knowledge throughout the company as it is also the alarm code for the building, and is used by the warehouse store supervisors and manager when they close up in the evenings.

Once inside the accounts office the working area is open plan, and anyone inside has full access to all the working areas.

### Your role – review and recommendations

The first job John has asked you to do is to review the accounting system and particularly the effectiveness of its internal controls.

You are then asked to make any recommendations for improvements which you feel are necessary. John knows there are many weaknesses – but is uncertain as to how these should be managed.

To help you in this he has asked the accounts clerks to prepare some brief information about themselves, an overview of the accounting system and also a list of events that have occurred over the previous few months. This information can be found below.

## ACCOUNTING STAFF

The current staff in the accounting office are as follows:

### Jo Doyle (Wages Clerk)

Jo is 24 years old and has been working for the company for four months. She is employed as a wages clerk and prepares the wages and salaries for all staff, along with all the associated returns, on a two day a week basis on a Wednesday and Thursday each week.

She has a young child, Harry, who is three years old, and spends all her free time with him. Though she is willing to work some extra hours if needed, she does not want to commit herself to any more permanent hours, as she would need to rearrange her child care.

Jo gained her AAT NVQ level 2 in payroll four years ago but has never progressed any further since due to the arrival of Harry.

### Gary Idawo (Accounts Clerk)

Gary is eighteen years old and has been working for Bayou Stores for just a year since he left the local 6th form college with three GCSE Advanced 'A' levels, including one in accounting.

His main responsibilities are as the accounts receivable (sales ledger) clerk and his duties include running all the trade credit accounts for the company. He works four days a week – and has chosen not to work on a Friday. This is because his main hobby is music, and he plays in a band every weekend – and Friday is his rehearsal day.

He has had no formal accounting training, but was trained on-the-job by the previous accounts receivable clerk before she left the company. He has, however, expressed an interest in learning, and wants to increase his accounting skills but is uncertain about how to go about this.

### Marion Smith (Accounts Clerk)

Marion is 57 years old and she has been employed at Bayou Stores for eight months. She has recently been widowed and decided she needed to return to work to supplement her income.

Her main role is that of accounts payable (purchase ledger) clerk. She is employed on a part-time basis of five half days per week, and she often likes to work these together to save on her bus fares to work. So for the past few months she has been working all day Tuesday and Wednesday and a half- day on Thursday morning.

She has several years experience in operating accounting systems, but has not worked in this area for over ten years, since she left her last role to care for her sick husband.

## ACCOUNTING OFFICE PRACTICES AND SYSTEMS

### Information Technology Systems

There are three computers in the office, as John has provided one for every member of the accounts team. These are all run on a stand-alone basis, though they are all linked to the same printer. Since John had some knowledge of Microsoft Office Excel spreadsheets whilst he was in the fire brigade (as they use this as their stock control system) – he has based the stock system for Bayou Stores on this same method and because of this the wider accounting system is also being run using Excel.

Two computers were purchased new when the company was established and are running on Windows Vista operating system; they are also loaded with Microsoft Office 2007 version (with a three user licence). Six months ago a further new computer was also purchased and loaded with Sage Payroll software to enable the payroll to be run in-house.

When the computer system was set-up a password was installed to protect the work. This is also UOYAB, as John uses the same security code for everything throughout the company because he feels this makes life easier.

### Wages and Salaries

Until six months ago the payroll was completed by the company accountants, Pearl & Johnson. However, this was beginning to become very costly, as the individual hours worked each week by staff are so variable that the payroll run was different every week, and the accountants charged for the time taken to complete this. John made the decision that the wages and salaries could be run in-house. For the first two months, he used a temping agency (but again this was an expensive option) to operate this, until four months ago, when Jo started working for the company.

All store staff are paid weekly, in cash, and pay packets are available from the store manager from 8am on a Friday morning. The office staff and store manager are paid monthly, by cheque, on the last working day of each month.

Store staff are paid a basic rate of £7 per hour for the first 40 hours worked and time and a half for any hours over this from Monday to Saturday. Any hours worked on a Sunday are paid at double time. The store supervisors, of whom there are four, are also paid the same overtime premiums but based on a basic rate of £9 an hour.

The supervisors are responsible for preparing staff rotas for their own departments to ensure that there is adequate staff coverage for all of the opening hours. Most of the warehouse staff are willing to work overtime, so this does not usually create any problems. Once the week has finished, the completed rotas are given to Jo who uses them to calculate the amount of hours that the individual store staff have worked.

Jo prepares the payslips from this information on a Wednesday, calculating manually any overtime payments due, and any Sunday working. From this, she calculates how much cash needs to be drawn from the bank and uses the company cheque book (which is kept locked in Marion's desk) to prepare a cheque ready for John's signature. On a Thursday she then prepares the pay packets, which are stored in the office safe for the store manager to collect, (though often it is the supervisors who actually do this), and to hand out to the staff the following day. Any pay packets not given out are returned to the office safe and remain there until collected by the relevant member of staff.

Only Statutory Sick Pay (SSP) is paid to the warehouse store staff, but the office staff are salaried and are allowed four weeks contractual sick pay per year.

John has always trusted his workforce completely and there is no requirement, or system in place, for either store or office employees to sign in when they arrive or leave work.

### Accounts Payable (Purchase Ledger)

All inventory (stock) is purchased on credit terms from a very wide range of suppliers. This is John's main role and he does enjoy spending time researching new stock lines, and also meeting the sales staff from different suppliers. He has a favourite group of suppliers he tends to use, mainly because the sales staff from these treat him to an occasional game of golf.

All inventory (stock) levels are maintained on the Excel spreadsheets. These have been set up to show suppliers, cost prices, selling prices, profit margins, and re-order levels and quantities. Marion has worked on Excel previously, but this was over ten years ago and whilst she is competent at inputting data, she sometimes struggles with anything beyond this.

Suppliers are paid at the end of the month that their invoice is received, as long as funds are available. However, due to the current credit crunch some suppliers are now beginning to request payment earlier, within thirty days of the date of invoice, and this is beginning to cause John some concern.

All suppliers are paid by cheque. These are completed by Marion, and the only authorised signatory is John. The cheque book is stored in a locked drawer in Marion's desk in the accounts office.

### Accounts Receivable (Sales Ledger)

Gary is responsible for the running of this function. Whilst many customers pay cash for their goods, over fifty per cent take extended credit terms. When Gary first started at Bayou Stores, anyone who applied for a credit account was accepted. However, he realised that this was not good practice and he now uses a credit reference agency to ensure that potential new credit customers have no history of poor payments. Other than this check any new customer who applied is automatically granted an unlimited line of credit.

All new credit accounts are set up on the first day of the month and Gary often works extra hours on this day to ensure this task is completed. All sales orders are received by the warehouse store staff for processing and, after completion, are passed to the accounts department the next morning, so that Gary can prepare the invoices and enter these in the accounts. Gary has designed a form in Microsoft Office Word which he uses as a pro forma for invoicing.

Bayou Stores offers sixty days credit to all their customers, and Gary is responsible for ensuring payment occurs. The policy on this is that once payment is seven days overdue Gary will telephone the customer. If payment is not received within seven days of the telephone call, then a 'stop' will be placed on the account and that customer is then not allowed any more goods or credit until payment has been made for any invoices more than sixty days old.

Gary allows two half days per month for the task of telephoning customers who are late in paying; drawing the information from an aged debtors control listing which has been set up on the Excel system to indicate customers whose accounts are outstanding for more than sixty days.

### Cash and Banking

Gary opens the mail every morning and sorts through it. Any cash or cheques received from customers are entered manually into a day book to record the receipt, which is then used to update the accounts. The cheques and cash are then placed in the office safe until a banking day.

At the end of every day, all cash and cheques are removed from the tills, leaving a float of £100 cash in each till for the start of the next day. The principle is that the till should be balanced to ensure that the cash content is correct, but during the week this does not happen as the store closes at 10pm, and the supervisors feel that they should not be asked to do an extra job at this time of the evening. Therefore, common practice is that all cash (except for the till floats) and cheques are removed and bagged as takings from individual tills before being stored in the safe in the accounts office.

Banking is carried out on a Monday and Thursday, and this is normally Gary's job which he does during his lunch break. The Thursday banking of cash is often lower as John has now started to reduce the cheques drawn for wages by the amount of cash available in the office safe on a Thursday morning. His idea is that any cash available can be used to supplement the making up of the wages to reduce the amount of cash needed to be drawn from the bank.

There is no petty cash system as such. If cash is needed for any incidental expenses, this is taken from the till floats and a note put in the till to cover this.

### DIARY OF EVENTS FOR THE LAST THREE MONTHS

### October 2009

One Tuesday, David Singh, a worker from the warehouse store, who has been off ill for five days, came into the office to collect his wages for the previous week, which he had not received due to his illness. His supervisor sent him upstairs to the accounts office, but even after a thorough search of the office safe, and then the office itself, the pay packet could not be found.

David was naturally annoyed at this and Gary tried to help. As Jo was not at work that day, and no one else could operate the Sage payroll system, it was not known how much David was owed. Gary decided that the rota said David was due to work 45 hours that week and so calculated his pay accordingly as:

35 x £7 plus 5 x £14 (Sunday working) plus 5 x £10.50 for overtime. Therefore, he thought David was due £367.50 – so he gave him this amount of cash from the safe.

Later in the month Gary caught flu and was off work ill for two weeks. He therefore did no credit control work during this time. Marion worked one day extra a week to cover his work – but could not manipulate the data, or access the pivot table on the Excel spreadsheet that Gary uses to highlight outstanding payments.

In an unheard of incident John has taken the last five days of the month off to attend a golfing tournament he has been invited to by a supplier. However, this was a last minute invitation and he only informed the accounts staff by telephone as he was on his way to the airport. He knew that he would need to pay suppliers during this time, and also staff wages, so he went to the office at 6am and signed a cheque book full of blank cheques to cover this. He had taken his spare keys with him, so was surprised when he discovered Marion's desk drawers unlocked.

On the last Friday of the month, Marion called into the office to pick up her salary cheque. As no one was about, and she knew that Jo had prepared these earlier in the week, she helped herself to this from Jo's desk drawer.

### November 2009

John told the accounts staff that after a telephone conversation with the bank manager he was very concerned over the size of the company overdraft and he had been informed that this must be reduced over the next four months.

He sat down with Gary to review he amounts owed by customers and was surprised to discover that more than twenty small retailers, who all are very good customers, owed more than £75,000 each. It became clear that they all take advantage of the full sixty day credit terms given by Bayou Stores and only make the minimum payment due, at the very end of this period.

During this meeting Gary asked John about undertaking some accounts training, and John says he was very happy for him to do this, and would be willing to pay for it, if Gary could locate a suitable course.

On the first Monday in the month an irate supplier again telephoned the accounts office regarding late payments, and threatening to withdraw Bayou Stores credit facility. As Marion was not at work, Gary took the call and promised the supplier that the cheque would be in the mail that evening. He knew where the cheque book was kept, and that the drawer was often left unlocked; he thought he could complete the cheque and ask John to sign it and send it to the supplier immediately. However, he discovered that there was still a blank cheque which had already been signed by John during his golfing break, so he completed this and mailed it to the supplier to ensure they are satisfied. He was subsequently busy that week and so forgot to inform Marion of his actions – and as each accounts staff member only normally works on their own computer, he did not update the accounts payable system.

On the second Friday in the month the telephone in the accounts department was ringing incessantly. At lunch time Stevan Teery, a warehouse store supervisor, went into the accounts office to answer it only to hear from a credit controller in a supplier company who was chasing up an invoice that had not been paid within their thirty day terms. Stevan could only try and placate the supplier, and take a message for the accounts office staff.

The following week, five warehouse staff complained to Jo that their wages were wrong. They had been asked to work extra hours to cover staff sickness, but this had not been marked on the rota sheets, and therefore they had been underpaid for the extra hours they worked. Equally it meant that the two staff who were off ill, had been overpaid for these hours but they had not reported this to the accounts department.

**December 2009**

Jo had booked two weeks holiday over Christmas, as she wanted to spend this time with Harry. As she knew that she is the only member of staff who can operate the Sage payroll system she decided to complete three weeks pay packets on the same date – all based on the hours worked in the current week. She completed the pay packets and placed them in the safe, informing the supervisors that Gary will give them out on the correct Friday and that any over or under payments will be adjusted during the following week after she has returned to work.

On the last Monday in the month a warehouse store worker, Matthew Perkins, came into the office to complain. Unbeknown to the other warehouse store staff he was having matrimonial problems, had recently left his wife to live with his girlfriend, and had taken a few days holiday last week for this move. His wife was aware that he was on holiday and had turned up at Bayou Stores and asked the supervisor for his pay packet saying that he was too busy to call in for it. As the supervisor knew his wife, (he had met her with Matthew at the staff Christmas party last year) he had handed her Matthew's pay packet without question, leaving Matthew with no money for the week.

**TASKS**

**Complete a business report to John Bayou**

This should be approximately 3500 - 4000 words long, and should cover the tasks set out below.

Note the references to the assessment criteria.

**Task 1**

**Complete a review of the accounting system**

This can be of the complete system or of one or more of the accounting functions, depending on your findings, but must specifically cover the following areas:

(a)     Record keeping systems - the purpose of financial reports, and the suitability of the organisation's current reports to meet organisational needs. (EAS 1.2  & PIC1.2)

(b)     Internal systems of control - identify how internal control supports the accounting system and the types of internal control in place, and any controls that are missing. (PIC2.4, PIC3.2  &  EAS 1.4)

(c)     Fraud - causes of fraud, common types of fraud, methods used to detect fraud and potential areas for fraud within the organisation. (EAS 1.4, PIC2.2 & PIC2.3, PIC 3.1)

(d)     Working methods/practices - including the use of appropriate computer software, and the operating methods in terms of reliability, speed and cost effectiveness. (PIC 3.4 & EAS 1.5)

(e)     Training (PIC 3.3) - Identify how training is or can be used to support staff.

The review should cover all aspects of the assessment criteria, as mapped above, when it can naturally be introduced into the report. If it cannot be covered in the report then it can be covered within a written explanation included in the appendix.

Whilst a SWOT analysis may be a good starting place, this should not be placed in the body of the report.

**Task 2**

**Identify weaknesses and make recommendations for improvement**

•       Once the review of the system has been completed, the weaknesses that have been identified should be clearly explained along with their impact upon the organisation. (EAS 1.3 & PIC 3.1).

•       For every weakness that has been identified there should be a recommendation made to attempt to improve the situation.  (EAS 2.1 & PIC 2.4 & PIC 3.2)

The recommendations should concentrate on the effect that the changes would have both on the organisation and on individual members of staff (EAS 2.2 & PIC 1.5).

They may also highlight training needs or aids to improve staff performance (EAS 2.3 & PIC 3.3).

**Task 3**

**Prepare a Cost Benefit Analysis**

At least one of the recommendations made should be subject to a cost benefit analysis. Whilst not all benefits are quantifiable, all costs are and students should make any necessary assumptions or 'guesstimates' to allocate costs to such items as time, unknown salaries, or any other unknown expense involved in the recommended changes.

All benefits should be identified, included those which cannot be allocated a financial figure. This can include such things as improved customer relationships, improved documentation systems or staff morale (though this could be allocated a financial benefit as improving staff turnover cuts recruitment costs). (EAS2.4)

**Note on Appendices**

Any charts and diagrams or supporting evidence should be included here and cross-referenced within the text.

Any appendices included should be referred to in the main body of the report or, in the case of supporting statements to cover missing assessment criteria, mapped and cross-referenced to a copy of the unit standards.

# Sample Student Reports

This Section contains sample material adapted and extracted from two original student Reports:

- Coro Scanning Limited – a manufacturer of electronic stock control devices

- SJT Logic (UK) Limited – a company which researches and develops satellite communication technology for the mobile communications market

The aim of this section is to provide guidance for the areas covered in a typical Report. A frequent question asked by students is "How do I get started?" – the problem being a lack of familiarity with what is required. It is hoped that the following pages may help.

These Reports are not claimed to be 'model' reports and you should not necessarily rely on the layouts shown as being definitive, but they give a good idea of what a report should look like and the issues raised when analysing an accounting system. You should note that:

- Format and style of presentation may vary (see page 66 for a recommended list of report sections).

- The Coro Scanning Limited report incorporates a cost-benefit analysis.

- Appendices have generally been omitted.

- Names and locations have been changed to preserve confidentiality.

# Sample Report 1:
# Coro Scanning Limited

*Note that each section of your Report should start on a new page. For the sake of economy of space and consideration for the rainforests this practice has not always been followed in this text.*

---

**INVESTIGATING AND IMPROVING THE WEAKNESSES IN THE ACCOUNTING FUNCTION FOR CORO SCANNING LIMITED**

Submitted by: Lara Stoddard

AAT student membership number: N002010

Date: March 20-2

This report is submitted for assessment of competence in AAT Learning and Assessment Area 'Internal control and accounting systems'.

---

**LIST OF CONTENTS**

*\*Note: these supplementary sections are not reproduced in this text, with the exception of Appendix (e), the SWOT analysis.*

## 1. TERMS OF REFERENCE

1.1 The report has been prepared to cover the requirements of AAT Learning and Assessment Area 'Internal control and accounting systems'.

1.2 The objectives of this report are to analyse the accounting function and to identify any weaknesses, and then to make recommendations for improvement.

## 2. METHODOLOGY

2.1 To begin this project the Office Manager (OM) had a broad look at the accounting function within CSL and identified key weaknesses in processes, software utilisation and time management. After finding these weaknesses the OM commented on possible solutions or ideas that could speed up processes, increase the accuracy and improve the utilisation of the software. (This can be seen in the 'Weaknesses and findings of the current system' section)

2.2 After outlining the weaknesses and commenting on possible solutions, these ideas were put to the Chief Financial Officer (CFO) in a meeting. The CFO and OM then decided to improve the Supplier payment process, as this would be one of the easiest to improve and would have a larger positive impact than if some of the other ideas were improved. (See appendix – f)

**References**:
• Osborne Books text: 'Internal Control and Accounting Systems'
• Sage manual and helpline
• Barclays helpline

**Acknowledgements**:
• Alex McFinlay – Chief Financial Officer
• Lynn Turberfield – Tutor, Trantridge College of Technology
• Chin-Shan Huang – Barclays Support Team

## 3. NATURE & STRUCTURE OF CORO SCANNING LTD (CSL)

3.1 Coro Scanning Limited (CSL) is a manufacturer of electronic stock control equipment which enables stock levels to be recorded remotely on a real time basis.

CSL's technology is widely applicable. The initial commercial focus is on the retail markets, enabling retailers to reduce operational costs and drive revenue increases through better stock control and more economical stock holdings.

3.2 CSL has three main suppliers that produce the components for its equipment. CSL also has many other suppliers that supply one off and rare products for the research & development department. CSL has two manufacturing companies that produce the final units. The main bulk of this is done in China with the finishing touches and dispatching done through a UK-based company.

3.3 CSL has many, mainly American based competitors all using similar technology to produce high devices to be used within the retail market. All these companies are at different stages within researching and manufacturing the technology. CSL is nearest to completion as manufacturing has already commenced on a low scale.

3.4 CSL is a company solely owned by shareholders. Each employee has a small number of shares while a board of investors own the majority.

The investors are the main decision makers in the company with the help of a hand-picked executive team, who all meet at a monthly board meeting.

The executives are in charge of running their own departments, reporting to the Managing Director (MD), who is in direct contact with the board throughout the month.

The main three departments are: Finance, Sales & Marketing and Research & Development (R & D).

These departments are then split down into separate areas according to the cost centre structure (appendix - a), where managers are appointed their own area and report to the executives. The organisational chart (appendix – c) allows employees within each area to see which department they belong to and and to whom they need to report. CSL's organisational structure is essentially flat.

3.5 The accounting function within CSL is a small department as seen in the cost centre structure and organisational chart (appendices – a & c). Its main tasks consist of preparing the daily books, producing month and year-end accounts according to the chart of accounts (appendix - b), managing budgets for R & D expenditure and other departments and obtaining funding from investors, venture capitalists and the government. As CSL is a small company the accounts department is also responsible for payroll, human resources and many other duties.

These tasks are split between the Chief Financial Office (CFO) and Office Manager (OM), controlled through regular meetings and checklists.

3.6 Lara Stoddard, the writer of this report, is the Office Manager (OM) of CSL. Lara carries out daily and monthly accounting tasks, as well as writing reports, running and organising the office, managing the purchase and sales ledger and paying suppliers.

Since starting with CSL in April 20-5 LS's career has already progressed from an Accounts Assistant purely inputting data to Office Manager with many responsibilities and in charge of many different areas.

## 4.    DESCRIPTION OF THE CURRENT SYSTEM

4.1    The supplier payment system currently operates every two weeks by BACS in order to pay outstanding invoices and expenses. This action is completed by using two different software packages, Sage 50 and Barclays Online Banking.

4.2    Sage accounting software is used to record all accounting entries from one year to the next and also allows you to monitor and control trade receivable & trade payable accounts, as well as many other uses.

For the supplier payment runs, Sage outlines the invoices that are due for payment with the use of a simple report, which is run by the OM. This allows a manual reconciliation between the outstanding invoices and the creditor balances on the report. Allowing all items being put forward for payment to be ticked as due for payment.

4.3    Barclays online software allows the user to see transactions in the form of a statement and transmit payments via BACS.

4.4    Once invoices have been checked against the outstanding creditors report from Sage, the OM puts forwards the outstanding invoices with a manual calculated total to the CFO for payment authorisation.

4.5    After the CFO has agreed with the OM for the invoices to be paid, the OM enters the amount to be paid for each supplier onto the Barclays system. All supplier details are saved onto the Barclays system so only new supplier BACS details have to be added and separately authorised by the CFO.

4.6    The OM requests the CFO to enter his authorisation code into the Barclays system once all details have been entered which in turn allows the OM to transmit payments with the use of another authorisation code.

4.7    Once the payments have been transmitted through Barclays, each invoice has to be posted as paid on Sage. This is done by the OM allocating each payment against outstanding invoices in individual supplier accounts.

4.8    The OM and CFO are the only two people involved in the payment run and also the only two people in CSL with the knowledge and authorisation codes to complete a payment run.

## 5. WEAKNESSES AND FINDINGS OF THE CURRENT SYSTEM

5.1 A SWOT analysis has already been carried out on the accounting function in CSL highlighting the Strengths, Weaknesses, Opportunities and Threats (Appendix - e [see pages 101-102]). From this it can be seen that there are the following key weaknesses in the supplier payment process.

5.2 **System Integration** – The Sage and Barclays software is not being used to its full potential during payment runs. Currently outstanding invoice information is manually sorted and payment details are entered on to Barclays followed by the invoices being posted as paid on to Sage, as explained in the 'Description of the current system'. Problems occur as information has to be entered twice in two different software applications. If there was a way of integrating the two applications and allowing them to talk to one another, information could then be sent from one application to the other. This will speed up the time it takes to complete the payment run and also reduce the amount of mistakes.

5.3 **Time Management** – As CSL only has a small accounting team made up of two people - the OM & CFO - managing a vast work load is very difficult, and any possible ways of improving processes to make them more efficient should be taken advantage of. Currently by entering the same data twice means that the accounting function is not working to its full potential. Therefore by improving the supplier payment process the OM will be able to save a significant amount of time that can be spent in other areas.

5.4 **Knowledge** – The current knowledge of Sage and Barclays software within CSL's accounting function is very limited, meaning neither of the applications is being used to its full potential. By learning more about both applications either through a training course, books or over the telephone, the accounting department will learn ways and means of speeding up processes involving Sage and Barclays such as the supplier payments runs.

5.5 **Processes** – Previously implemented processes are becoming out of date for many reasons and need to be updated to increase the efficiency of CSL's accounting function. Processes may have fit in to the accounting function before as there was previously more staff and less work. They need to be updated to fit into the current accounting function, which is made up of only two people carrying out more and more work as the company grows. Processes such as the supplier payment process, which previously fitted in well and didn't seem a problem, now feel like a waste of time that could be considerably speeded up by cutting out unnecessary tasks.

5.6      These four factors outline the main problems affecting CSL's accounting function. The supplier payment run process is one of the most obvious tasks that could be improved with useful results, due to it being repeated at least twice a month and includes aspects that could easily be cut out and improved with a little more knowledge and understanding.

5.7      Not only does the payment run process waste time that could be spent on other tasks but it also makes the OM inefficient because she must regularly enter the same data twice when time could be spent on more important tasks.

## FINDINGS

5.8      After meeting with CSL's CFO to discuss the possible weaknesses of CSL's accounting function (appendix – f). It was concluded that the supplier payment run process was the best process to concentrate and improve on first. Other tasks discussed in the meeting will be looked on again in the future when they become more of a priority.

Reasons for this were that out of all the processes completed in every month the supplier payment process was one of the most common and would therefore result in the OM saving more time than she might have saved by reviewing other processes such as month end.

It was considered the best way to find out about integrating Sage and Barclays to gain the most out of both software applications was to learn more about both software packages from their handbooks and also call both help lines to ask for advice.

5.9      Less time wasting, money saving and job satisfaction were the three key benefits that were agreed in the meeting, which would be improved by increasing the efficiency of the supplier payment process, thus benefiting the company, the CFO and the OM. These were good reasons to go ahead with the task and make as many improvements as possible.

**6.      RECOMMENDATIONS**

6.1      After deciding to improve the supplier payment system and having spoken to representatives from Sage and Barclays, it was decided that there was only one viable option to speed up the process. This was to implement a file exporting system from Sage to Barclays carrying all the payment data and bank details within it.

To decide if this was a worthwhile project the OM carried out a Cost Benefit Analysis.

6.2      **Cost Benefit Analysis** – This has been carried out to identify the monetary savings by increasing the efficiency of supplier payment runs.

Current Process –

- 3 hours is the time to complete data entry for payment submission on Barclays and record invoices as paid on individual supplier accounts.

- £8 p/hour is the cost of the OM's time.

- Twice a month is the average amount of times a payment run is completed.

Total cost per month (3 x £8 x 2) = £48

Total cost per year (£48 x 12) = £576

Improved Process –

- 1 hour is the time taken to pick the payments from Sage as paid and transfer data to Barclays.

- £8 p/hour is the cost of the OM's time.

- Twice a month is the average amount of times a payment run is completed.

Total cost per month (1 x £8 x 2) = £16

Total cost per year (£16 x 12) = £192

Benefits –

- £32 per month

- £384 per year

- 4 hours per month

- 48 hours per year

6.3      After assessing the benefits it is clear that by improving the efficiency of the process both time and money is being saved, meaning it can be spent better on other tasks.

Freeing up over a week's worth of the OM's time in a year will allow the OM to spend time on other areas of the business such as sales. This will become a substantial new task added to the existing OM role.

### 7.    FRAUD

7.1    There is a possible opportunity for fraud to take place within CSL, as some of the controls within the accounting function are very weak. It is not currently a huge problem as there are only two staff and controls are sufficient. This may not be the case in the future when more staff are employed by CSL and more people have access to the accounts package. This means that the system will have to be re-evaluated and either replaced or updated in conjunction with the changing situation.

7.2    Fraud levels are constantly increasing within businesses due to many factors including:
   • Growing complexity of organisations
   • Understaffing and lacking in Internal Audit Functions
   • Outdated and ineffective internal controls
   • Aggressive accounting practices
   • Little or no segregation of duties
   • Increasingly transient employees

7.3    Fraud is defined as a deliberate deception to secure unfair or unlawful gain.

   There is not currently a known issue with fraud within CSL's supplier payment system but if there was it could possibly occur because of the small size of the team and a lack of segregation in duties, together with a lack of controls within Sage.

7.4    The new supplier payment system involves the OM exporting payment data from Sage to Barclays once all invoices have been authorised by the CFO.

   The following problems could possibly occur:
   • The OM enters all invoices onto Sage and reconciles the data at the end of the month. There is a possibility for fraud by setting up and paying a fake supplier.

   • The OM also reconciles the bank statement at the end of the month and could cover up any false payments or expenses before sending the final reconciliation to the CFO.

   • The OM enters all supplier details (ie address, VAT number & bank accounts) onto Sage to allow online payment data to be exported. There is no control when entering the bank account information in Sage. This could allow the OM to enter any bank details.

7.5    The only controls preventing this are that the CFO must type in his password on Barclays before any payments can be transmitted and all bank details entered onto Sage are also recorded in a spreadsheet available for the CFO to randomly check at any time. Unfortunately these controls are very weak as they rely on the CFO double-checking all payment information that has been recorded by the OM. In theory these are acceptable procedures but in real life the CFO does not have time to double check all the payment data the OM has entered and ultimately relies on trusting the OM to correctly enter all information.

7.6 There is also a possibility of collusion between the CFO and OM, as it is such a small team it would be possible to join together and 'steal' large amounts of money from CSL's bank. This could occur as nobody else in the company has access to the bank accounts and the only figure reported to the executives, the board of directors and investors is what is written in the CFO's monthly management report.

7.7 Minimising the risk of fraud is done by understanding why and how it occurs. It is important to identify areas that are at risk and implement procedures to address these vulnerable areas. A key control in minimising the risk of fraud relies on segregation of duties within the department.

This is therefore difficult for CSL to do in the current situation but as the company grows, systems and procedures will be put in place to maximise duty segregation and minimise possible chances of fraud. Future recruitment of accountancy staff should also be looked at very carefully, making sure staff are trustworthy and are not given access to all data from the start but only data that is necessary for them to carry out their duties.

**Appendix (e)**

**SWOT ANALYSIS**

**STRENGTHS**

- **Small team** – CSL has a small accounting function made up of two people, thus making it easy to control and manage.

- **Good communication** – Regular meetings are held to allow good communication within the accounting department. This allows everybody to clearly understand what tasks they must complete and their role in the overall picture.

- **People** – The accounting function contains people with the appropriate skills and qualifications to carry out their job role to a high standard.

- **Resources** – CSL's accounting function has the availability of many resources, allowing the company a smooth progression to becoming a large organisation.

**WEAKNESSES**

- **System integration** – Systems within CSL's accounting function are not used to their full potential, such as Sage accounting and Barclays online banking.

- **Time management** – Managing a vast workload within a small team can be very difficult and time may not always be managed correctly. Systems could be implemented to improve this, such as checklists to prioritise tasks.

- **Knowledge** – Not understanding the full potential of software and systems hinders the efficiency of the accounting function. Courses and reading up on the software and systems being used, can improve knowledge.

- **Processes** – Previously implemented processes are becoming out-of-date as the company grows. By identifying this weakness and implementing training in specific areas, these processes can then be updated to suit the needs of the company.

**OPPORTUNITIES**

- **Business sector** – CSL's business sector is expanding with many future opportunities for success.

- **Industry or lifestyle trends** – CSL has forecasted the industry and lifestyle trends to allow its technology to fit in and be adapted if needed.

- **Development and innovation** – CSL's technology has the opportunity to be developed into hundreds of different applications depending on markets and demand.

- **Partnerships** – CSL has set up key partnerships with large organisations already key players, such as Novitsu. This gives CSL instant credibility in the market.

**THREATS**

- **Competitors** – CSL's main competitors are American-based companies at similar stages in the product development. CSL is in a race against these companies to roll out their products earlier and faster than anyone else.

- **Political effects** – As noted in my PEST analysis (appendix – d), CSL has the potential threat posed by many political factors, especially within China where CSL's manufacturing plant is based.

- **Market demand** – The success of CSL depends entirely on the market demand for its products. Demand is very difficult to predict, especially overseas where CSL aims for the main sales to take place.

- **Economy** – As covered in my PEST analysis (appendix – d), there are many economical factors that affect the future of CSL, especially during the R & D stages.

# Sample report 2:
# SJT Logic (UK) Limited

*Note that each section of your Report should start on a new page. For the sake of economy of space and consideration for the rainforests this practice has not always been followed in this text.*

---

**THE IMPLEMENTATION OF A NEW AND IMPROVED ASSET TRACKING LIST TO REDUCE ERROR AND TIME SPENT BY EMPLOYEES**

Submitted by: Victor Bruno

AAT student membership number:  N017654

Date: March 20-2

This report is submitted for assessment of competence in  AAT Learning and Assessment Area 'Internal control and accounting systems'.

---

**LIST OF CONTENTS**

*Note: these appendices are not reproduced in this text.*

**1      TERMS OF REFERENCE**

1.1    This report has been prepared to cover  AAT Learning and Assessment Area 'Internal control and accounting systems'.

1.2    The objectives of this report are as follows:

- To identify the weaknesses in the current system used to track assets at SJT Logic (UK) Ltd.

- To recommend the implementation of a new and improved system to reduce errors, stop potential fraudulent activities and save the time of all users.

**2      EXECUTIVE SUMMARY**

2.1    To summarise: after research and feedback from employees within SJT Logic it was decided that a new database could be created to track the assets for the company.

2.2    This would include a full sweep of the building for missing assets and assets without asset labels.

2.3    This was to be done to save the time of all employees trying to track down items on the asset register, whether for a financial or research purpose.

**3      METHODOLOGY**

3.1    It was apparent there were issues with the existing asset tracking, so to pinpoint specific errors a questionnaire was distributed to a selection of employees from all departments who use the tracking system on a regular basis.

Once the results were analysed it was clear that a drastic change in procedure was needed to save the valuable time of the employees.

3.2    A meeting was arranged with the accounts manager and the engineering manager to discuss all the options and to decide the way forward for the asset tracking system. Once the new system was to be put in place employees would be encouraged to give feedback on the use of the new database.

**Acknowledgements**

3.3    Thank you to all the people who took the time to complete the questionnaires.  Also thank you to the managers who agreed to discuss a plan of action.

**4      ORGANISATIONAL BACKGROUND OF SJT LOGIC (UK) LTD**

4.1     SJT Logic (UK) Ltd is a research and development company based in Radbrook, Cambridgeshire. Its parent company is SJT Logic USA based in Sacramento, California.  SJT researches and develops satellite communications and supplies its systems to the mobile communication market. It has built, and is continuing to build, a network of communication in the air, across land and across sea that is second to none.

4.2     SJT Logic USA is a quoted company and is owned by shareholders from around the globe and these include its employees.  SJT has a mission statement that says it is committed to delivering superior value to its customers, share holders and employees as a trusted supplier of advanced products and services to the mobile communications and emergency market.

The SJT Logic core values are as follows:

• Integrity

• Individual respect

• Professionalism

• Commitment

• Accountability

• Passion for continuous improvement

4.3     The United States Department of Defence (DOD) is the biggest competitor in the communications market. The US Government controls around 60%, the other 40% is privately controlled.  Trion and Chelton (a division of Cobham Omnipless) are two of SJT Logic's biggest private competitors.

4.4     Honeywell, Rockwell Collins, Thales, Spanish UAV, the USA MOD and the French Navy are some of SJT Logic's biggest customers.  SJT Logic uses many different suppliers for their components and expertise from around the world.  SJT Logic also has many suppliers that are also customers. In these cases, different pools of knowledge are combined together to develop certain products, which will be a benefit to both parties.

In Appendix 2 there is an Organisation Chart showing both the UK and USA companies.

A PEST Analysis showing the Political, Economical, Social and Technological Factors effecting SJT Logic is filed in Appendix 3.

**5      STRUCTURE & FUNCTION OF SJT LOGIC (UK) LTD**

See Appendix 1 for Org. Chart

5.1     SJT Logic is a hierarchical or "tall" structure.  It has series of levels of people and each level is controlled by the level above. This is very typical of such a big organisation where each level is centralised and strictly controlled.

5.2     The organisation is mainly sub-divided according to function into the following areas:

- Engineering and Business Development

- EMP Product Support

- Product Management

- Engineers

- Product Development

- Tracking and Messaging Systems Sales

- Logic (UK)

- Broadband Sales

- Marketing

- EMP Sales

- Business Operations

- Business Process

- Field Services


**Corporate Services:**

5.3     The accounting function is a small section of the Logic UK structure.  It contains Keith Masters (KM) as the Finance and Operations Manager and Victor Bruno (VB) as HR/Finance Coordinator.  VB reports to KM who in turn reports to Jan Vilic (JW), VP Business Operations.  The management team based in the UK is made up of a director, KM, the UK engineering manager and a manager of business development.

5.4     VB's role as the HR/Finance Coordinator includes preparing all sales and purchase invoices, making payments, processing received payments, overhead analysis reports, forecasting, project recharges and sundry recharges, asset tracking and absences from work.

See Appendix 4 for a SWOT Analysis.

## 6 EXISTING ASSET TRACKING SYSTEM

6.1 As assets enter the building they are checked in by the lab technician Anne Fellowes (AF). AF checks items against documentation either the delivery ticket or the original purchase order (PO).

6.2 The assets are then distributed to the person who first raised the PO or to the end users depending on what term it is.

6.3 VB must then locate the item when the invoice is received for the goods and attach an asset tag, which has the company logo on and a sequential number.

6.4 VB records the asset number, current location, make, model and serial number in the excel asset tracking spreadsheet.

6.5 If they are capital items (a high value item where the cost is spread over a period of time in the accounts) they are also recorded on the Asset Register.

See Appendix 5 for an example of the existing Asset Tracking System.

## 7 STRENGTHS AND WEAKNESSES OF EXISTING SYSTEM

7.1 There are a number of weaknesses that have been identified in the current Asset Tracking System:

- Assets can be in the building for up to a month without being recorded. This does not give a true picture of the company's assets.

- Assets can get missed so they in effect do not "exist" at all. The costs are absorbed within the individual project and so items can be missed.

- It is time-consuming for VB to find assets once they have been distributed.

- Items could be vulnerable to theft as missed assets do not "exist" in the records.

- The Excel Spreadsheet is incomplete therefore making the tracking system pointless.

- The Excel spreadsheet is not very user friendly. It is very time consuming.

- Other information about the assets, for example the warranty and calibration records, are all kept in separate places allowing for errors and miscommunication.

- Assets on spreadsheet are not all current; disposals have not been recorded accurately. This means that not all records match.

- All assets are lumped together; there is no distinction between departments, making it harder to find items.

- Local information is out of date since many changes have taken place in the layout of the building. This makes finding assets a lot harder for the employees.

7.2 Motivation is important because it encourages people to work well. Effective motivation of employees means providing them with variety of work, chances to make their own decisions, the feeling their job has value and elements of challenge. A lack of motivation usually leads to long, unauthorised breaks, poor quality of work and reluctance to work.

The current asset tracking system de-motivates employees because it does not add value to their work, it also does not enable employees to achieve their goals. This is a major weakness of the system because it encourages poor quality of work or a reluctance to work at all.

## 8 STRENGTHS

8.1 There are several strengths in the current asset tracking system, although these are significantly fewer than the weaknesses.

- All users know where to find the spreadsheet on the system.

- All users know how to use Excel.

Excel is installed on all computers within the company.

8.2 All these strengths and weaknesses should be considered when the recommendations are made for improving the system.

## 9 FRAUD

9.1 Fraud covers a wide variety of offences but in general terms fraud is seen to be the use of deception with the intent of obtaining an advantage, avoiding an obligation or causing loss to someone else or an organisation. Fraud is a criminal activity.

9.2 As mentioned in the weaknesses of the asset tracking system, it is currently an opportunity for theft. As not all assets are checked and tagged as they enter the building they could easily be taken by employees. It would then be very difficult to trace these assets because a formal procedure has not been put in place.

9.3 Also, as the information on the current tracking list is not up-to-date, items that have been stolen would not immediately be picked up. As asset disposals are not always notified to VB and therefore not always recorded on the tracking list, it could be assumed or made to look like these items have been disposed of legally rather than actually stolen.

**10   FINDINGS**

10.1   A questionnaire was distributed to employees in all departments that use the existing asset tracking system.  All employees who were given a questionnaire completed it.

See Appendix 6 for details.

10.2   It was overwhelmingly clear from the feedback received on these employee questionnaires that no-one was happy with the existing tracking system.  All seven employees surveyed agreed that the information was not easy to use and was incomplete and/or irrelevant.

All employees suggested additional information that should also be included.  The engineers unanimously agreed that the tracking system should also contain calibration and warranty information, thus no longer duplicating information in other spreadsheets.  Both Product Support (IT) and the Operations team agreed that splitting the assets into groups would aid them when tracking assets.

10.3   All employees who completed questionnaires agreed that in the existing system not all the information was relevant and not all items are tracked in the spreadsheet.

**11   IMPROVING THE SYSTEM**

11.1   There are four suggested options for improving the asset tracking system. These are listed below:

(1)   Update the existing Excel spreadsheet and take out columns that it has been decided are irrelevant.  Make every effort to add all new additions to the spreadsheet by better communication between staff.

(2)   Create a new Excel spreadsheet with pivot tables and make sure all data carried over from the existing spreadsheet is correct.  Again, make every effort to track down new additions.

(3)   Create an Access Database that is user-friendly when using look ups by creating a front switchboard with searches. (See Appendix 9 for an example).

Make all columns relevant and incorporate all asset information including calibration and warranty.  Group assets into 3 groups, Admin, Computer Equipment and Engineering.  Again, ensure that all new additions are tracked down.

(4)   Change the procedure for receiving goods so that all goods go to VB before AF checks and distributes them so asset tags are already attached, and then record them in the Access Database mentioned in Option 3.

After a discussion was held with the managers about all the available options for improving the asset tracking system a list of Pros and Cons was created for each option.  These are detailed below (see next page).

11.2 **Option 1: Update the Existing Spreadsheet**

Pros:

- Quick and simple
- Fewer man hours
- No cash outlay

Cons:

- Does not cover the calibration and warranty issues
- Does not make it more user-friendly
- Theft is still possible
- Time is wasted by VB having to locate assets
- The company's records are not always up to date due to the time delay in asset tagging items

11.3 **Option 2: Create a New Spreadsheet**

Pros:

- More relevant than the existing spreadsheet
- Easy to do
- No cash outlay

Cons:

- Not user-friendly for its purpose
- Theft is still possible
- Time is wasted by VB having to locate assets
- The company's records are not always up to date due to the time delay in asset tagging items

11.4 **Option 3: Create an Access Database**

Pros:

- User-friendly searches
- Assets in different groups can still be linked by searches
- All information will be relevant
- Easy to use

Cons:

- Cost in time for creating a database
- Outlay for Access training disk
- Not all users have Access installed on their PCs
- Theft is still a concern
- Time wasted by VB having to locate assets
- The company's records are not always up to date due to the time delay in asset tagging items

**11.5    Option 4: Change Goods in Procedure and Enter Data into the Access Database in 11.4 (see previous page)**

Pros:
- User friendly searches
- Assets in different groups can still be linked by searches
- All information will be relevant
- Easy to use
- Theft will be minimised
- Time saved by VB not having to locate assets around the building

Cons:
- Cost in time for creating a database
- Outlay for Access training disk
- Not all users have Access installed on their PCs

# Index

**for your notes**

**for your notes**

**for your notes**

**for your notes**

**for your notes**

for your notes

**for your notes**

122

**for your notes**

**for your notes**

for your notes